The PSYCHOLOGY of CHARACTER BUILDING for AUTHORS

Using Psychological Principles to Design Unforgettable 3D Characters

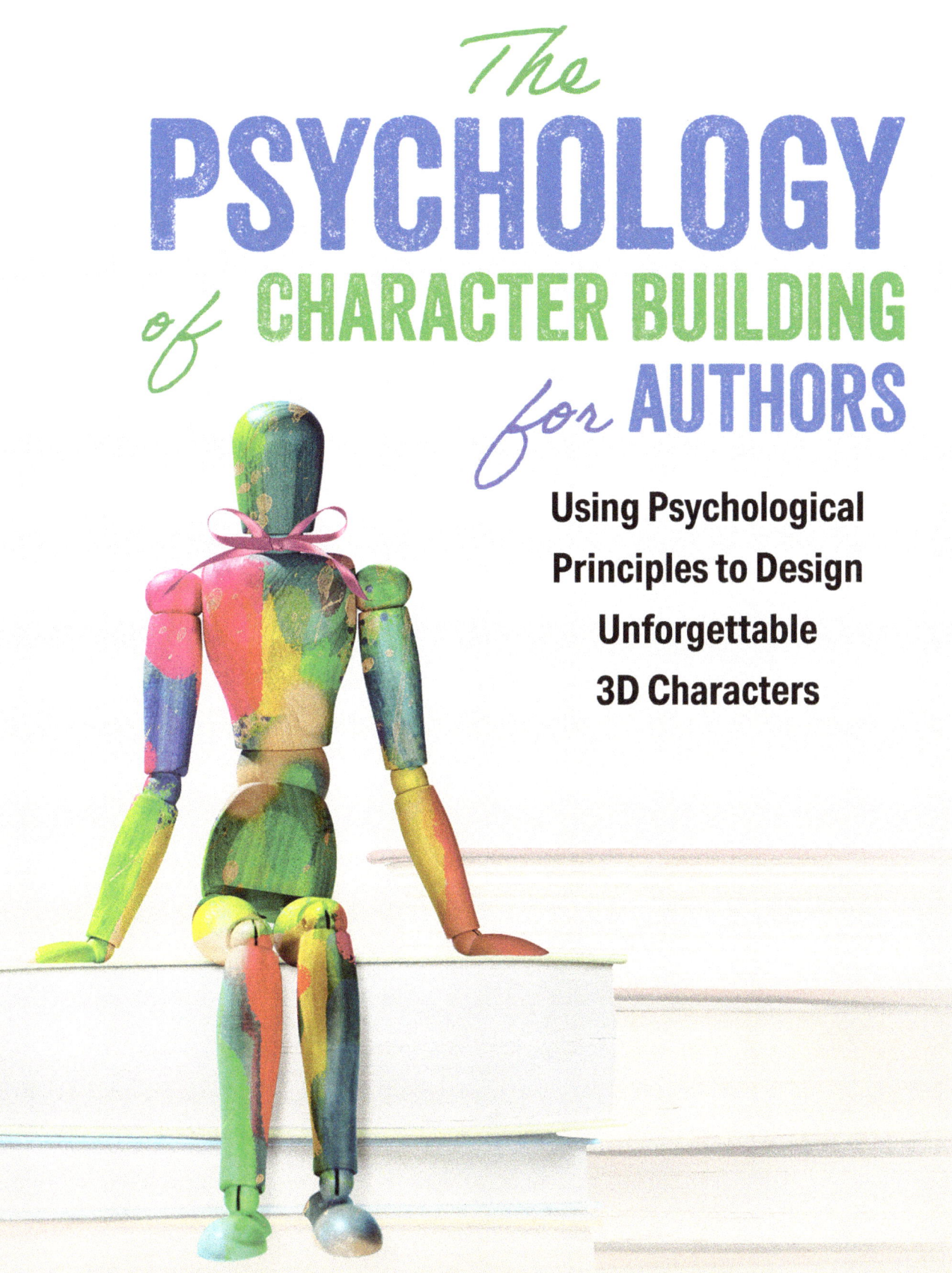

The PSYCHOLOGY of CHARACTER BUILDING for AUTHORS

Using Psychological Principles to Design Unforgettable 3D Characters

LETITIA R. WASHINGTON, MA

The Psychology of Character Building for Authors
Copyright © 2022 Letitia Washington. All rights reserved.

Accomplishing Innovation Press
1497 Main St. Suite 169
Dunedin, FL 34698
accomplishinginnovationpress.com
AccomplishingInnovationPress@gmail.com

Typesetting by Niki Tantillo
Edited by Blair Parke

All rights to the work within are reserved to the author and publisher. No part of this publication may be reproduced, stored in a retrieval system, or transmitted in any form or by any means, electronic, mechanical, photocopying, recording, scanning, or otherwise, except as permitted under Section 107 or 108 of the 1976 International Copyright Act, without prior written permission except in brief quotations embodied in critical articles and reviews. Please contact either the Publisher or Author to gain permission.

This book is meant as a reference guide. All characters, organizations, and events portrayed in this book are a product of the author. All brands, quotes, and cited work respectfully belong to the original rights holders and bear no affiliation to the authors or publisher.

Library of Congress Control Number: 2022942215

Paperback ISBN-13: 978-1-64450-682-0
Hardcover ISBN-13: 978-1-64450-683-7
Ebook ISBN-13: 978-1-64450-681-3

To the 3D characters who are waiting to have their authentic stories told, and the writers who want to connect with them.

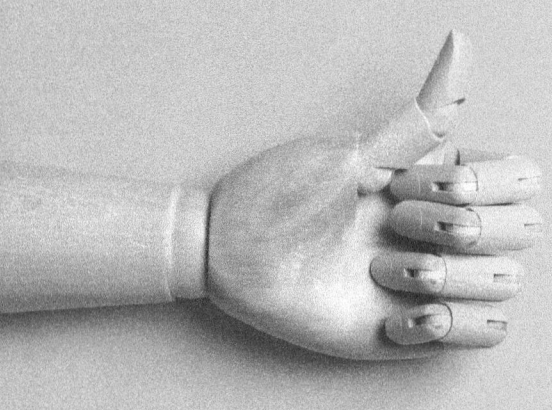
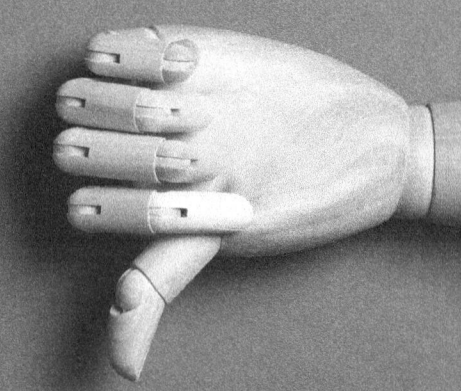

WHAT THIS BOOK IS

This book is a tool that will help you, the author, think about your characters as living, breathing creations, who possess rich backstories and colorful experiences—not robotic, cardboard cutouts that don't have minds, feelings, or emotions of their own.

You will explore your characters' emotional and psychological struggles, as well as their trauma, to connect with them in a way you might not have been able to before.

For this book and the techniques discussed to be successful, you will need to tap into your imagination and apply psychological principles to the process of character development.

You are about to take an exciting adventure with your characters, discovering new things about who they are.

Be open to this process, and I guarantee you will see a difference in your writing by the time you have finished reading this book.

WHAT THIS BOOK ISN'T

DISCLAIMER: This book is **not** a degree in psychology and does not give you permission to practice therapy on family, friends, or even pets. Psychology is a very specialized and important profession that requires years of training and countless hours of practice to truly fathom. Additionally, this book is not a replacement for real counseling or therapy.

If you or someone you know is in distress, contact your local psychological service provider or crisis hotline.

HOW THIS BOOK WORKS

While psychology might be a challenging subject area for some, my goal in writing this book for authors is to make the concepts easy to understand and apply. With this in mind, the book has been split up into **four sections**, which include subsections to explore topics such as:

1. **Setting Up the Canvas:** a review of major established concepts in character development.

2. **Getting Psychological:** a crash course introduction to psychological theories and concepts.

3. **Applying Psychology to Character Design:** how to apply the previously discussed psychological theories and concepts to character design.

4. **Pulling it Together:** streamlining the character development process.

Once you have finished reading each section, you will be invited to consider a three-step process that will allow you to become a well-oiled, character-development machine.

If you have questions or would like coaching regarding how to apply these concepts, do not hesitate to contact me: info@brooklynknightauthor.com

TABLE OF CONTENTS

How This Book Works vii
Introduction 1

Section I

Chapter 1
Setting Up the Canvas 7

Chapter 2
Archetypes 12

Chapter 3
Character Arcs 17

Chapter 4
Goal, Motivation, & Conflict 20

Section II

Chapter 5
Getting Psychological 24

Chapter 6
Chief Emotional Themes 27

Chapter 7
Psychology 101 32

Section III

Chapter 8
Applying Psychological Theory
to Character Design 44
Conclusion 65

Section IV

Chapter 9
Psychological Tools 70

Author Bio 149
References 150

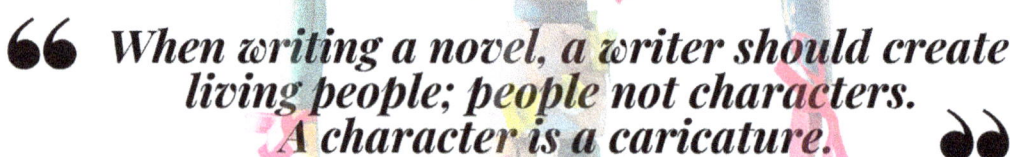

> *When writing a novel, a writer should create living people; people not characters. A character is a caricature.*

ERNEST HEMINGWAY

INTRODUCTION

Character development is not a process authors should take lightly. This is my heartfelt position, and I've been contemplating this thought for a while, probably since I published my debut novel under my pen name "Brooklyn Knight" in 2018.

What made me consider this topic so deeply?

Maybe it's because I'm a trained clinical mental health counselor, and I've been conditioned to care about people and the sometimes stressful, day-to-day task of being alive. I'm also a people-watcher, and for as long as I can remember, I've been interested in how humans self-actualize (or don't). In my work, I've engaged tons of children and adults (both singles and couples) in the process of identifying the sources of their trauma and coming up with solutions to their problems in a therapeutic environment.

Maybe it's something else.

Maybe it's because, according to the Clifton Strengths Assessment, a tool that helps individuals identify and build upon their strengths, one of my top five strengths is *Relator*, which means I have the ability to connect with people on a deep, emotional level.

Not only this, but apparently (and I find this to be true), I do this behavior with real people as well as with the characters I create. I develop relationships with my characters so I have the ability to *be* in touch with their emotions and effectively convey them from my head onto the page.

No, this isn't a hocus-pocus, woo-woo manual—you purchased the correct book. The point is I'm good at understanding people, and I learned to translate this into my ability to create compelling, 3D characters for my novels. In the beginning, I wondered why I had such a knack for developing characters, but then, one day, it all started to make sense.

The other day, I was being interviewed on a podcast. The host had read one of my popular romance novels and was curious to know how I'd developed it. She said she read the blurb, instantly clicked on the title, and was amazed at how invested she was in the hero's journey. She then asked how I was able to craft such a believable character when many authors struggle with the task.

My response surprised her.

I told her it was easy because I genuinely know my characters.

Like, *really know* them.

They are real people (or things) to me.

They have dreams and visions that do not belong to me.

They have wants, needs, and motivations that have nothing to do with who I am as the author, and it's up to me to:

1. Know what these wants, needs, and desires are and

2. Get them onto the page in a way that authentically tells their stories and represents who they are.

Essentially, it's not about me, and after I took up the task of becoming a storyteller, I realized that it never was. My job as the author is to tell *other* people's stories, and if you're an author, then it's your job as well. Unless we're writing a personal memoir, we have no business imposing our dreams onto these unique characters and selling it as fiction. It is incumbent upon us, as authors, to tell our characters' stories in fresh, compelling, and unforgettable ways—and that starts with us knowing who they are, both inside and out.

There are so many moving parts that are incorporated into a good story; no author worth their salt will deny this. A story is a meticulous combination of circumstance, character, drive, desire, motivation, challenges, obstacles, hurdles, mountains—the list goes on, so I'm sure you get the point. But of all the things that go into the pot of "what makes a good story," I'm of the opinion that *character* is the most important ingredient; and while some authors may believe plot to be the heartbeat of the story, I'm here to suggest otherwise.

It's character.

Don't get it twisted—without a good plot, your story would literally remain in stasis, but without powerful, multifaceted characters, who would want to take the journey and accompany them through hardships?

For this reason, your characters—*all* of them, from the hero to the villain and the sidekick—need to be larger than life! Their larger-than-lifeness may not make it onto the page, since not every detail of their life will be relevant to the plot; but if you know how amazingly turmoiled your characters are, so will your reader and they will want to travel with them to the ends of the earth and back.

How Do I Know?

As I said, when it comes to designing characters, I've developed a knack for it. I know this because during my bi-annual exercise of taking

stock of my reviews and defining their themes (something I do to gain an understanding of what readers say I'm doing right, as well as what they think I could be doing better), I discovered something amazing.

Here are a handful of my reviews. See if you can spot the trend I unearthed.

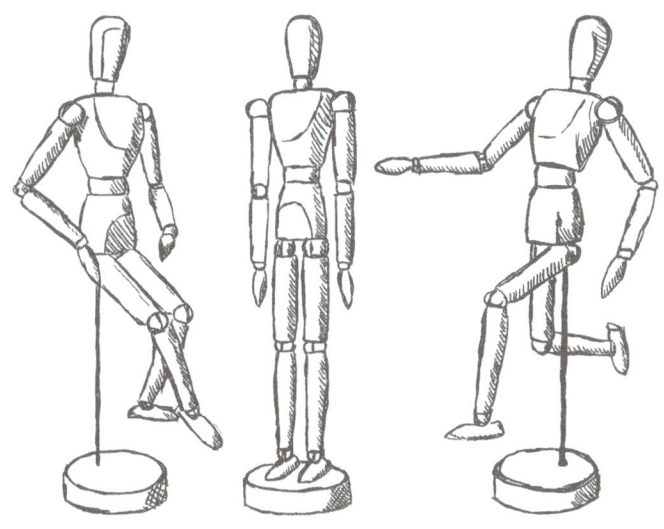

> This book was amazing it had me on the edge of my seat from the beginning to the end. I just love Remi and Roman.
> —5/5, *Goodreads Reviewer*

> The writing draws you in and keeps you involved throughout the whole story, I found myself in love with not only the characters but also the world that was created. The descriptions of the characters and their feelings are so involved, you can truly picture it in your mind. Their attitudes toward the events that are happening makes the story even richer.
> —5/5, *Amazon Reviewer*

> I was getting so worried throughout the story. I really thought I was going to lose one of my favorite characters from the first 3 books. I had come to admire him and I really didn't want to see his demise. So glad for the turn the authors took.
> —5/5, *Goodreads Reviewer*

> Heavens know waiting was hard for part two of their story, but so worth it. To have a love that deep, to have someone who is incomplete without being near that person so much so that they would die, it became so easy to get caught up in their love. It's great story.
> —5/5, *Amazon Reviewer*

Do you see what I see?

Five-star reviews are awesome, as they almost always tend to be. These readers shown here are raving about one of my ominous and sexy heroes, and based on what they said, they connected with him and could feel his excruciating pain. Allegedly, I was able to transport these readers into his very mind and emotions. They could see and feel everything he saw and felt as he was seeing and feeling it.

They wanted him to be in love! They wanted him to win, and they wanted all of these things for him because they were familiar with his heartache. They felt as if they knew him, and this happened because I knew him first!

From a thematic standpoint, these reviews (and tons more) are commenting on the same thing: character. What's more, they're all speaking to how deeply and intensely the readers felt connected to my characters. Some of them hated him, while others (thank God most, as of this writing) loved him beyond measure. But when the rubber meets the road, it doesn't matter whether readers loved or hated him. What matters is that this character was able to evoke emotions in the readers, one that influenced them to write a review and pushed them to get the next book, and the one after that as well.

> ***Tip***
> Have a look at your reviews and see what themes you can uncover.
> What are your readers telling you about how they like your book and/or characters?

Now we have some evidence of what happens when you design compelling characters, and perhaps, like the woman who interviewed me for her podcast, you're curious about how I approach the task in its fullness. If so, let's discuss a few psychological principles and meet our characters in such a way that makes them unforgettable, both to ourselves and our readers. But first, let's review the general principles of understanding who our characters are inside.

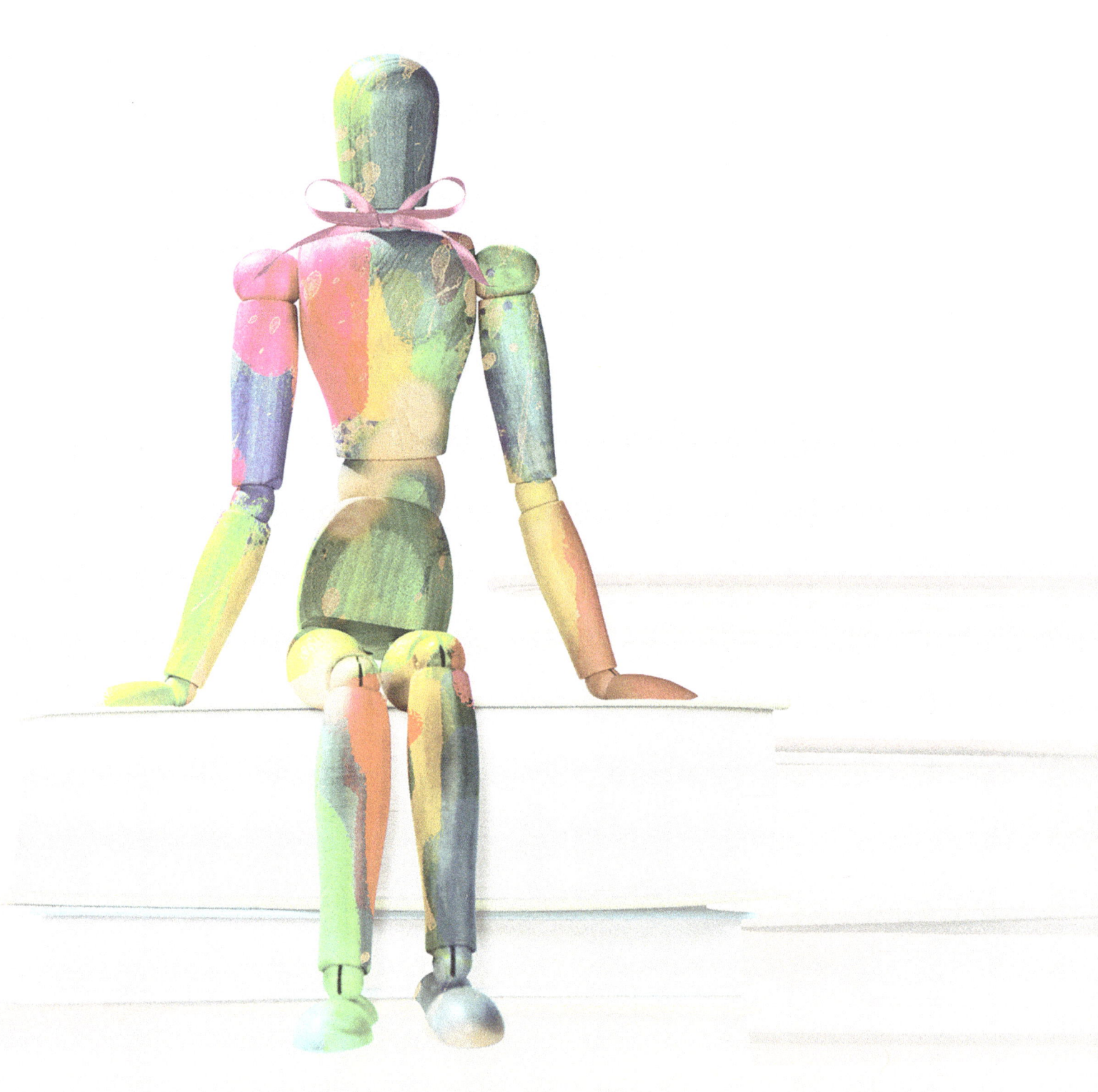

Chapter 1

SETTING UP THE CANVAS

Before we get deep, down, and dirty into the psychology of our characters, it's important to know the basic information regarding who they are.

Fun fact: this is also true in the therapeutic setting.

Whenever I was assigned a new client as a counselor, the first thing I'd get was a file highlighting their basic demographic information (think name, age, date of birth). This allowed me to establish a working knowledge—a foundation, if you will—of who the client was prior to talking to them. It also gave me rich context for when the not-so-obvious details about who they were started to come out.

The same is true for character design. Before you can begin to explore your character's psychology, you need to know the basics of who they purport to be. This often equates to the things others have told them and has nothing to do with their inner thoughts and feelings. That's the part we're going to uncover with our new psychological tools!

In this section, we're going to look at the foundation of character. Specifically, we're going to discuss:

1. The seven characters that should be in every story

2. Character archetypes

3. Character arcs

4. Goal, motivation, and conflict (GMC)

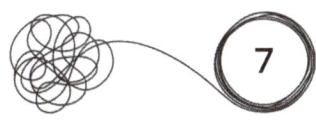

The Psychology of Character Building for Authors

Seven Characters to Include in Every Story

(Yes, Every Story)

If you think of the greatest stories ever written, it's not long before you realize each of them boasts a colorful and robust cast of characters. Classics such as *Anna Karenina* (Tolstoy), *To Kill a Mockingbird* (Lee), and *Don Quixote* (Miguel de Cervantes), which are touted as being tales to last the ages are due, in part, to the fact that their main characters have strong supporting casts behind them.

When it comes to our stories, this should be *our* goal—to surround our heroes and heroines with friends and foes who will make them shine.

I once read that every great story should include each of the characters I'm about to highlight. I have attempted to apply this advice to my personal writings (especially my full-length works) and have found that each of these characters play critical roles in the development of the story and character arcs.

Without further delay, here are the seven characters that should be included in every story (no matter the genre).

NB: *Some sources refer to eight characters, but I've combined two of them—tertiary and flat.*

1. Protagonist (Hero/Heroine)

2. Antagonist (Villain)

This is the main character in the story—the one the reader follows and roots for. The protagonist is the one who has the most extensive and fulfilling character arc. They are brave and courageous, and though they aren't perfect, they are compelling and must resonate with your readers.

The antagonist is the bad guy or girl—the evil one. He or she is the one who poses challenges for your hero or heroine. The villain should be evil and a little bit better than your hero (that's what makes the conflict so delicious); however, the key to creating an amazing villain is not making them 100 percent evil.

Is anybody 100 percent anything?

Give your villain a relatable characteristic that will play on your readers' sensibilities. Make them volunteer at a homeless shelter or feed stray cats every Wednesday.

Make your reader love to hate your villain!

4. Tertiary (Flat) Characters

Tertiary characters are those who have important roles to play in the story, but once they've fulfilled their purpose, they are off the stage. In the movie remake of *Jumanji*, starring Dwayne "The Rock" Johnson and Kevin Hart, a tertiary character was the young boy who gave The Rock's character the map. He literally conveyed a critical piece of information and was gone—we never saw him again! Yet, without his role, the plot would not have moved forward. This tertiary character was not an integral part of the overall storyline, but he had an important part to play.

3. Deuteragonist (Sidekick)

Wherever your hero goes, his or her trusty sidekick is right next to them. The sidekick is the guy or gal who hands your hero the sword and offers words of encouragement in their darkest hour. The power and importance of the sidekick should never be underestimated, and it's worth it to craft this character with as much care and attention as you do the protagonist.

I love sidekicks and almost always have readers messaging me requesting the sidekick get a story of their own. This is a byproduct of creating 3D characters—readers will want more!

Tertiary characters are also flat, which means the reader doesn't need to know or care about them. Whether they ate cold cereal or omelets for breakfast is unimportant, as is whether they came from a single-parent household or are trust-fund babies—nobody cares.

In essence, tertiary characters are like non-player characters (NPCs) in video games.

Think of the bartender who gives your hero his whiskey while he's sitting at the bar during the critical choice moment, or the Uber driver who gets your heroine from Point A to Point B. Adding details about these guys would bog the storyline down and make readers sigh with boredom.

5. Love Interest

As the name implies, the love interest is the character your protagonist has strong feelings for. Typically, the love interest is another major player in the story (think romance genre); however, it's entirely possible for the love interest to be a tertiary character (think any genre that doesn't rely on romantic elements to move the plot forward).

6. Mentor

The wise mentor is the character who gives your hero or heroine advice and guidance along their journey. Oftentimes, the mentor is the one who holds the key to the main character's success. Whether the main character knows it at the time of impartation is another matter, but they will certainly remember it during the dark night of their soul.

7. Narrator

This is the voice in your book—the person (or persons) who is relaying the narrative to your reader. Depending on your writing style (as well as what your character wants—you'll learn more about this in the upcoming sections of the book), the narrator could be in first-, second-, or third-person perspective.

First-person narration is when your character is the one telling the story. Essentially, this limits the tale to what your character sees, knows, and feels: however, it can be a powerful form of narration, especially if you, as the author, are tapped into your character's emotional GMC (again, we will touch more on this in the following chapters). Examples of books which have successfully utilized this POV form might include *Memoirs of a Geisha* by Arthur Golden or *The Kite Runner* by Khaled Hosseini

It should also be noted that it is common to include two first-person narrations in the same story. (I do it quite frequently.) This is called **dual-POV** and is perfect when you want to give the reader more than one character's perspective. Examples of dual POV books include *One Night on the Island* by Josie Silver and *Good Girl Complex* by Elle Kennedy.

Setting Up The Canvas

Second-person narration is rarely used, so I'll skip over discussing this one, but know that it can be used, typically in literary forms of writing and self-help books. It is not common elsewhere. Examples of books written in second-person are *Damage* by A.M. Jenkins and *The Fifth Season* by N.K. Jemisin.

Finally, **third-person narration** occurs when there is a neutral narrator. That is, the narrator can see everything and speak to what all characters are thinking and feeling (third-person omniscient); or they can stick with one character and tell the reader things the character notices (third-person limited); or the narrator can be completely neutral, which means they have no knowledge of what any character thinks or feels—they are simply observers, just as the readers are (third-person objective). To get an idea of what third-person narration sounds like, check out *Lord of the Rings* by J. R. R. Tolkien or *The Godfather* by Mario Puzo.

> *Tip*
> Whenever I discuss this topic with my students, I love to use the cast from the classic movie Annie. Watch the movie and identify each of the characters. Yes, all seven/eight are present!

> *Tip*
> Use the Seven Characters worksheet in the Psychological Tools Section to keep track of your characters as you write your book.

Chapter Recap

1. There are the seven characters:
   - Protagonist [Hero/Heroine]
   - Antagonist [Villain]
   - Deuteragonist [Sidekick]
   - Tertiary [Flat]
   - Love Interest
   - Mentor
   - Narrator

2. Each character should show up in *every* story, no matter the genre.

3. Your character will tell you who the narrator should be.

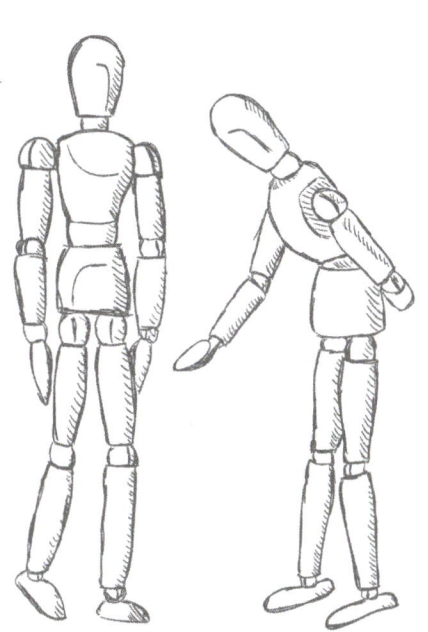

Chapter 2

ARCHETYPES

In the previous chapter, we discussed the seven characters you should always include in your stories. Here we're going to briefly consider archetypes, a concept which was developed by influential psychologist Carl Jung in 1947.[1]

According to literary form, there are twelve archetypes. An **archetype** is a pattern or theme that recurs enough to be considered universal. For example, when you hear the word "wizard," perhaps you think of Gandalf in *Lord of the Rings* or Harry Potter. Furthermore, said wizard must possess certain omnipotent qualities. These are all results of the archetype associated with the "wizard." Similarly, as an "explorer," Indiana Jones meets our subconscious requirements to be bold, fearless, and adventurous.

The characters you create will inevitably fit into one of these archetypal structures. Since this is the case, it's also important to know that each archetype possesses strengths and weaknesses that will undoubtedly be displayed over the course of your story.

Because this is a universal rule, some creatives might be afraid of creating cliché characters who fit into predefined molds—characters the world has seen a million times.

How *unoriginal* would that be?

But rest assured, a savvy writer will not experience this problem. What's more, a writer who is able to tap into the psychology of their character (the way you're going to learn in this book) won't have to worry about it either.

That said, to continue building on our character development foundation, let's look at the archetypes, as well as the strengths and weaknesses associated with each, so that when we conduct our therapy sessions, we can better understand who our character is. Many books have been written about this subject, so feel free to conduct an online search to learn more. In the meantime, here are the twelve archetypes and their associated strengths and weaknesses:

[1] (Nerher, 1996)

Archetypes

1. The Lover

This character is the hopeless romantic who is led by their heart, not their head. In romance, it's pretty obvious who this character (or characters) is; however, the Lover can be in every novel, no matter the genre.

Strengths: humanism, passion, conviction.
Weaknesses: naïveté, irrationality.

2. The Hero

This is the character who saves the day! They are the one who slays the dragon and brings the villain to their knees. The reader is rooting for this character, from beginning to end.

Strengths: courage, perseverance, honor.
Weaknesses: overconfidence, inflated ego, too trusting.

3. The Magician

This character understands the mysteries of the universe and has harnessed special powers to help them achieve their goals.

Strengths: omniscience, omnipotence, discipline.
Weaknesses: inflated ego, corruptibility.

4. The Outlaw

This character is a rebel, the bad boy/girl. They live on the edge and shirk the law, and they don't give two f@$%s about it!

Strengths: independent, owes no one.
Weaknesses: self-absorbed, prone to criminality.

The Psychology of Character Building for Authors

5. The Explorer

This character is adventurous and is driven to explore the unknown. They have no reservations and aren't fearful, even though others might be.

Strengths: curious, motivated, driven by self-improvement.
Weaknesses: easily bored, unreliable, never satisfied, risk with their life/lives of others.

6. The Sage

This is the wise character who knows everything. The other characters sit at their feet and glean from their knowledge.

Strengths: wisdom, experience, insight.
Weaknesses: cautious, ambivalent about joining the action, can be secretive.

7. The Innocent

This is a morally pure character (often a child) who only has good intentions. This character is incapable of doing any wrong and only sees what's right in the world.

Strengths: morality, kindness, sincerity.
Weaknesses: vulnerable, naive, rarely skilled.

8. The Creator

This character is a visionary who builds something tangible during the story (art, structures, etc.).

Strengths: creativity, willpower, determination.
Weaknesses: single-mindedness, lack of practical skills, self-absorbed.

Archetypes

9. The Ruler

This character has legal or emotional power over other characters in the story. They may hold high-ranking positions in society or within the family hierarchy.

Strengths: status, resources, influence.
Weaknesses: out of touch, often disliked by others, indifferent, prideful.

11. The Everyman

This is a relatable character whom readers will immediately identify with. Readers will see a piece of themselves in the Everyman.

Strengths: relatable, grounded, stable.
Weaknesses: lacks special powers, unprepared for the future.

10. The Caregiver

This is the character who is always supporting other characters in the story, even at their own expense.

Strengths: Selfless, loyal, dependable.
Weaknesses: Lacks personal ambition, lacks leadership skills.

12. The Jester

This character provides comic relief, but also reveals central truths related to the storyline, thus making their role critical.

Strengths: funny, disarming, insightful.
Weaknesses: can lack boundaries, can be superficial.

***

When working to create 3D characters, it is possible to take these archetypes and amplify them by thinking about the biopsychosocial model and applying psychological theories to them (we're going to talk about this in the next chapter). For example, what if our character, whom we know is the Jester, has not experienced unconditional, positive regard? Or what if the Caregiver has sacrificed so much of him/herself that they develop a codependent relationship and has attachment issues? How will this play out in the pages of your story?

Another question to consider is what happened to your character that forced them into their archetype? Why is the Ruler *the ruler*? Why is the Outlaw *the outlaw*?

Questions like these are examples of how we can go deeper into the character development process.

Don't worry if you don't know the answer to these questions yet. Keep reading, and you'll learn how to identify your character's trauma and apply it to your writing.

Chapter Recap

1. There are twelve archetypes: the Lover, the Hero, the Magician, the Outlaw, the Explorer, the Sage, the Innocent, the Creator, the Ruler, the Caregiver, the Everyman, and the Jester.

2. Question how your character came to fall within this archetype. What happened to them to make them the Caregiver (for example)?

3. How are your characters' strengths and weaknesses related to their personalities?

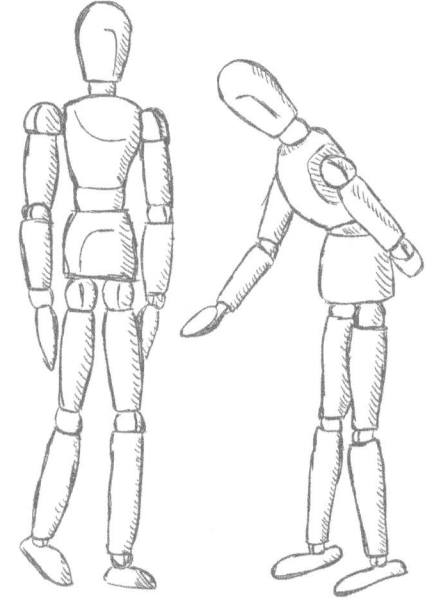

Chapter 3

CHARACTER ARCS

Before we launch into our characters' deep, subconscious thoughts, we need to be reminded of what creative writing theory says about the ways their thoughts develop over the course of a story in the first place. This is where the **Character Arc** comes into play, a representation of how your character will change over time in your story.

In the graphic to the right, your character starts off in **Status Quo Mode**—they have preconceived beliefs, which have been developed by their experience of the world, thanks to the effects of nature (biology, or genetically inherited traits/abilities) and nurture (sociology, or the way they were raised).

However, when your character encounters the *inciting incident*, they are launched into a circumstance that somehow challenges their previously held assumptions. Because they are no longer in their comfort zone, they are thrust into a journey to seek answers to the new questions that have been raised. The journey (your story) will present them with opportunities to change (new status quo).

The Psychology of Character Building for Authors

Different Kinds of Arcs

1. Growth Arc

A growth arc isn't necessarily a *complete* change or transformation. By the end of the story, your character is still the same person but they have overcome something within themselves. They are a better, more rounded person, or simply different in some way. In a growth arc, your character has changed their perspective, learned something new, or has possibly assumed a different role by the end of the story.

2. Transformation Arc

When your character enters a transformation arc, they undergo a complete change from "regular" person to hero or savior. This kind of arc is typically reserved for the protagonist, who is usually the underdog when the story starts. Over the course of the story, they experience a radical transformation, through which they discover an inner strength, talent, or drive they didn't know they had. This arc is common in fantasy/sci-fi genres but can be applied to any genre.

3. Fall Arc

As the name suggests, the fall arc is a negative arc that involves the decline or "fall" of a character, as a result of the choices they've made. This is ultimately the cause of their demise (and potentially the demise of others). By the end of this arc, the character has usually either died, become corrupted, or lost their mind (or, if they're lucky, all three). This is a great arc to apply to your villain!

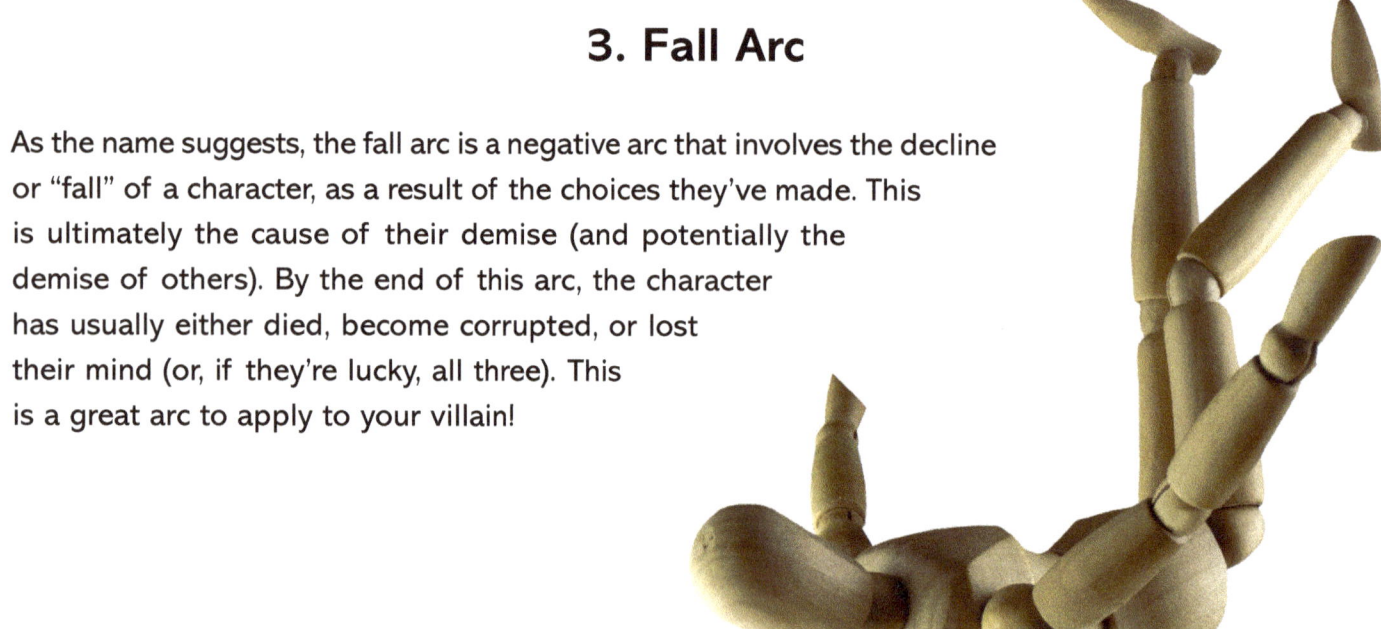

Character Arcs

Author Questions

1. Which arc is applicable to your main character?
2. Which arc is applicable to your villain?
3. What did your main character believe about the world on page 1 of your story? What do they believe by the end of the book?

Tip
Use the character arc tracking form in the psychological tools section to identify the changes that will occur in your character(s).

Chapter Recap

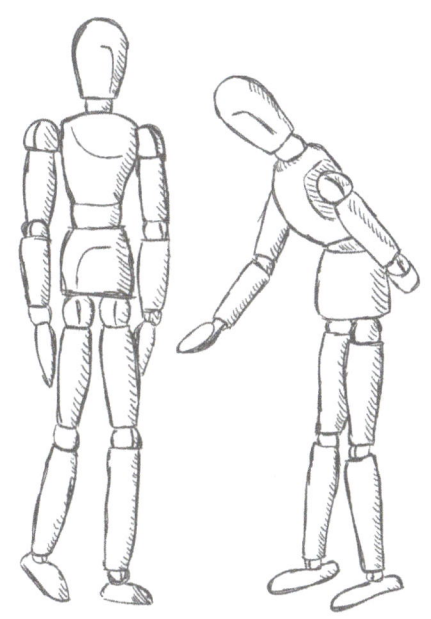

1. The character arc dictates that your main character should change in some way by the end of your story.

2. There are three kinds of arcs: growth, transformation, and fall.

3. Fall arcs are typically reserved for villains.

4. Transformation arcs are typically reserved for heroes in fantasy novels.

5. Without an appropriate character arc to follow, readers may be dissatisfied and give you a one-star review.

Chapter 4

GOAL, MOTIVATION, & CONFLICT

If you've been writing for any length of time, you know what *GMC* stands for (and no, it's not related to a motor vehicle company). **Goal, Motivation, and Conflict** are said to be the building blocks of knowing what drives our characters.

From birth, these factors are present. An infant has a goal (to be fed, to feel warmth, to be nurtured) and is motivated to achieve it, lest it experiences psychological and emotional distress (which is frequently evidenced by crying). However, there are times when said baby will experience conflict, some barrier that will prevent it from reaching its intended goal—the bottle isn't ready (or there's no food in the house); the heater is broken (or the electricity has been cut because the parental figures have lost their jobs and haven't paid bills); the parents are busy (or they've abandoned the child on the side of the street).

THINK ABOUT IT
How would any of these experiences impact your character within your story?

This is an example of GMC at its inception, but you should understand that it never ends. Adults are driven by GMC on an hourly basis, and the sum of the decisions we're required to make shape our personalities and the ways in which we interact with the world.

Thus, the **goal** is the thing your character is striving to obtain from the moment they hit the inciting incident. The rule of thumb is that your character's goal must be compelling enough that readers are willing to journey with them until the end of the book, watching, waiting, and praying they are successful in getting it.

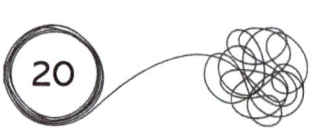

Goal, Motivation, & Conflict

By contrast, the **motivation** is the why behind the goal. In other words, why does your character need this thing? What is at stake if they don't get it? Will they lose the love of their life? Will someone close to them die? Will the world end? Your character's motivation is the thing that fuels him or her along the tumultuous journey. It is important to ensure that the stakes are high. This way, the reader will be invested in the storyline and your character.

Finally, **conflict** is the thing standing in your character's way—the thing that is blocking them from achieving their goals, which is fueled by their desperate motivation. This is the thing that keeps readers turning pages, as conflict is essential in a compelling story. The villain (whether a physical person, a force of nature, or a psychological impediment) must present your character with enough drama that by the time they reach "the end," the victory is well-earned for them.

Don't make it easy for your character either. The tougher the journey, the sweeter the reward (and the reviews for you)!

Later in this book, we're going to dig deeply into the idea of GMC by dissecting it into distinct parts.

Chapter Recap

1. The **Goal** is the thing that your character is striving to obtain from the moment they hit the inciting incident.

2. The **Motivation** is the why behind the goal.

3. The **Conflict** is the thing standing in your character's way and blocking them from achieving the goal.

4. Don't make it easy for your character. The tougher the journey, the sweeter the reward.

> *Your character will be what you yourself choose to make it.*

JOHN LUBBOCK

Chapter 5

GETTING PSYCHOLOGICAL

We've reviewed the foundational material in the last few chapters, which provide us with a great understanding of how characters come to be in the first place, but to design dynamic 3D characters, we will need to go a little deeper.

In this section, we're going to:

1. Gather some basic **Demographic Information** about our characters, which will serve as a springboard for our psychological inquiries into them.

2. Review the **Chief Emotional Themes** I've noticed in my work with real clients.

3. Consider seven **Psychological Theories** and principles, which we will use to dig into our characters' sub-consciences. This is for the purpose of uncovering pearls within the rubble of their trauma to make our stories more colorful.

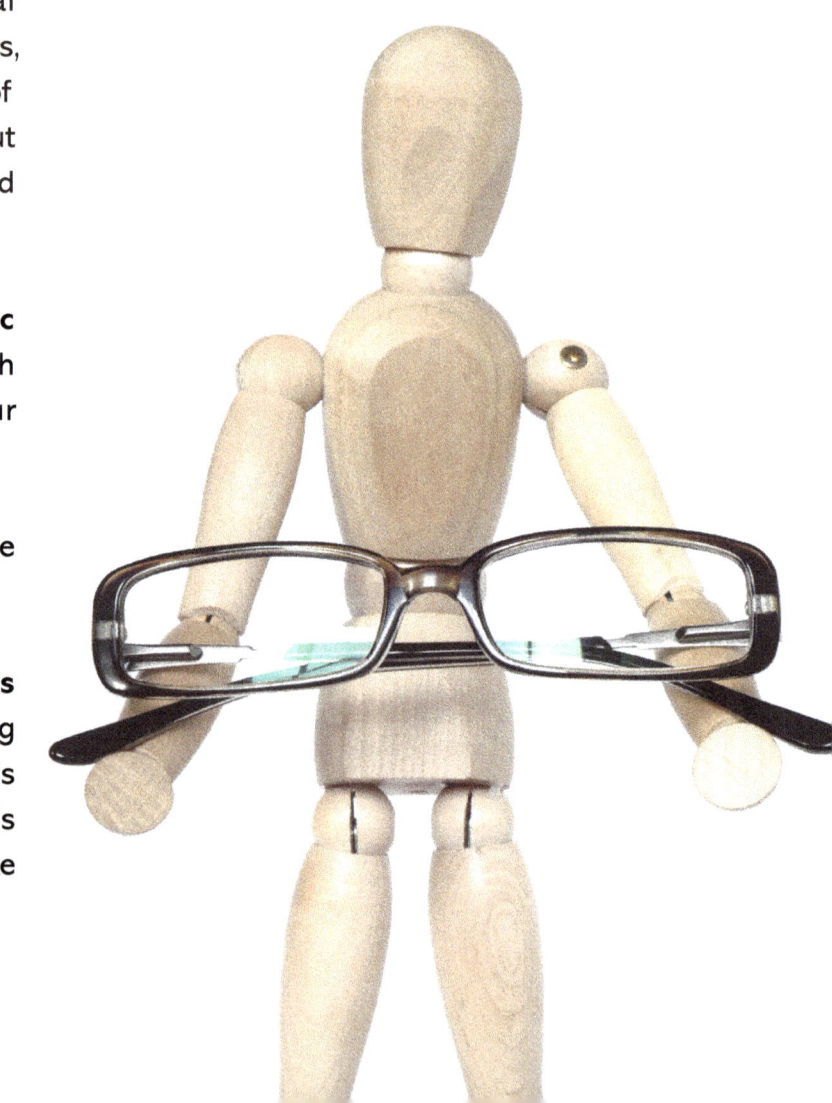

Getting Psychological

Demographics

In psychology, there's a thing called the biopsychosocial model. It's a long word (and as I've typed it, my word processor has conveniently highlighted it as not being a real one), but when you break it down, it makes complete sense.

Let's split it up.

Bio refers to an individual's biology—their genetics, the stuff they're born with and cannot avoid. These might include factors such as the way the character's brain works.

For example, some authors design heroes who are autistic or cognitively challenged (think Winston Groom's *Forrest Gump*). Another example might be a character who is involved in a car crash and loses their legs. As a result, they develop new self-esteem issues that prevent them from entering the dating world or achieving personal goals.

From a biological standpoint, characters like these were either born with or have sustained some physical characteristic that impacts how they view and interact with the world.

Psycho references the character's psychology, concerning the ways in which the character thinks, emotes, or behaves. For example, a character who is extremely self-conscious might believe that all the other characters in the story are talking about them. This might cause the character to be defensive or develop anxiety, which keeps them inside for the rest of their life.

In romance novels, you often find female leads who have been hurt in past relationships. As a consequence of this experience, their psychology prevents them from being open to Prince Charming when he pops onto the scene. This has also been done with heroes, where they are rough around the edges and don't really know how to treat the woman of their dreams because they've been emotionally scarred in some way.

Finally, **Social** is concerned with the character's circumstance and environment, and how it impacts their thought processes. Questions such as how the character grew up, their social status, or how much money they make come into play. Are they entitled? Do they turn their nose up at those less fortunate? Are they poor and blame others for their misfortune?

I recently read a novel that expertly discussed the ways in which a character's exposure to childhood sexual trauma forced him to develop split personalities or dissociative identity disorder (DID)[2]. The entire story was based on how the two sides of this character interacted with his love interest. Mind-boggling!

Perhaps the reasons why the theorists strung these three words (biopsychosocial) together is obvious to you. If it isn't, that's okay. It will all make sense by the time you finish this book. For now, understand that these three dimensions of a person (and your character) collide to create the sum of who they (and you) are. In other words, we are all the product of our biology, psychology, and social circumstances.

In this book, we're going to focus heavily on the psycho and social parts of this word, but it's also important to remember everything that happens to your character has the ability to impact how they view the world of your story.

---

[2] American Psychiatric Association. (2013). *Diagnostic and statistical manual of mental disorders* (5th ed.). https://doi-org.ezproxy.frederick.edu/10.1176/appi.books.9780890425596

CHARACTER QUESTIONNAIRES

You've probably seen tons of them; essentially, they are documents designed to examine the biopsychosocial factors as they relate to your character. A good character questionnaire will include questions that explore each of them. A great character questionnaire will prompt you to not only answer these questions with one-word responses, but also go deeper and consider the factors leading to these answers in the first place. It will require you to consider the *'why'* behind your answers, thus allowing you to be creative with your character development process.

If you haven't bumped into a comprehensive character questionnaire before, have no fear—I have one for you in the Psychological Tools chapter at the end of this book.

But we need to go deeper, and to do that, we must explore our characters' traumas and consider the ways in which they impact their biopsychosocial standing.

If you're ready to learn the techniques, read on.

Chapter Recap

1. All people (and characters) are the sum of biological, psychological, and social influences.
2. The term biopsychosocial refers to biology, psychology, and sociology (social influences).
3. Bio: genetics, brain function, physical and physiological limitations.
4. Psycho: the ways in which the character thinks, emotes, or behaves.
5. Social: the character's circumstance and environment, and how it impacts their thought processes.
6. A *good* character questionnaire will include questions that explore each of these domains.
7. A *great* character questionnaire will prompt you to go even deeper by requiring you to consider the *'why'* behind your answers, thus allowing you to be creative with your character development process.

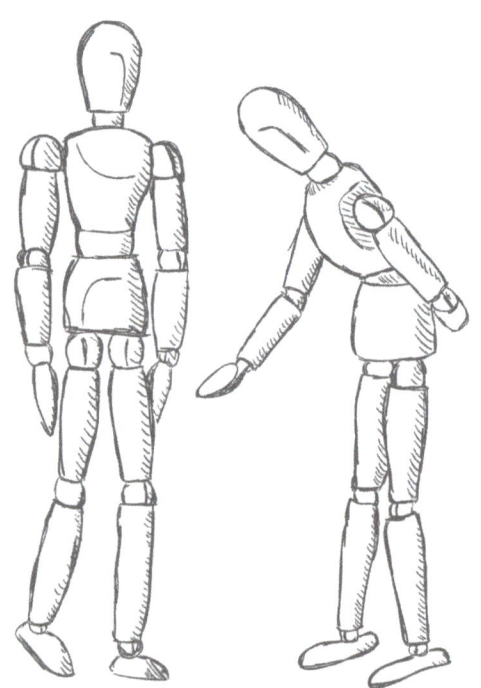

Tip
Use the character questionnaire in the Psychological Tools section to develop these three domains for your characters.

Chapter 6

CHIEF EMOTIONAL THEMES

Before quitting my job to write romance novels, I was a third-year PhD student at a reputable university, which saw me doing my doctorate in counselor supervision and education from 2015 until 2018. Prior, I obtained my master's in clinical mental health counseling, and before that, I achieved my bachelor's degree with a major in psychology and a minor in sociology.

Good times!

No, seriously.

Since 2013, I have had the privilege of working with adults, children, and families on a plethora of developmental, emotional, and mental health issues, ranging from the common diagnosis of ADHD to the more severe diagnosis of schizophrenia. Believe me when I tell you this work required high levels of trust, understanding, and compassion between myself, as the therapist, and my clients. As a therapist, my goal was to partner with these *real* people and journey with them into the depths of their vulnerability and trauma, for the purpose of guiding them back into the marvelous light of health and healing.

But my adventures with people didn't start there.

Before becoming a clinical mental health therapist, I was a probation officer for five years. This role found me in the heart of the jail cell, both literally and figuratively. I met people who committed heinous crimes and worked with others who were strung out on illicit substances. My task was to uncover the roots of their addiction and assist with the development of strategies to heighten my clients' chances of future success—a daunting role indeed. In most cases, these individuals disappointed others as well as themselves because of choices they'd made, and while working in this field can often seem like a thankless job, there were many silver linings.

Here is one of them.

While I was working with these *real* people, aiding them in the process of self-regulation and emotional homeostasis, something wonderful was happening for me. I was getting an in-depth look into the multi-layered nature of personality. I saw it all! I was face to face with all manner of issues, from narcissism, borderline personality, and attachment disorders to dissociative identity disorder and schizophrenia. While encountering these diagnoses served me well in my day-to-day line of work with clients, I later realized that it had also served me in my work with the ones I created—my characters.

Even though my clients' backstories were many, I was able to recognize themes in my work, just like I did with my five-star reviews. In other words, no matter who I saw or what their presenting issue was, I somehow was able to lump them into having one of five emotional categories. It should be noted that these categories are not directly related to any psychological principles or theories. Rather, these are the emotional umbrellas I discovered while working with multiple clients, helping me to better understand their complex issues and formulate solution-focused responses.

Let's check them out.

1. **Unconditional Positive Regard**
2. **Validation**
3. **Self-Worth**
4. **Inflated Ego**
5. **Abandonment**

1. Unconditional Positive Regard

This is a beautiful, clinical term, which basically means, "no matter what you do, I'm not gonna stop loving you." For many of my clients, they had not experienced this. Bridges had been burned (and rightly so for some of them), promises had been broken, and trust didn't exist anymore between them and their loved ones (some of whom were/are primary caregivers). The lack of unconditional positive regard opened the door for all kinds of trauma and neurosis to be experienced.

2. Validation

Clients who were on drugs or displayed other behavioral and emotional challenges often experienced a lack of validation from others who were important in their lives. They could never do anything right, as their thoughts, beliefs, and feelings were seen as worthless. Because of this experience, they often turned to drugs and/or other maladaptive behaviors to cope.

3. Self-Worth

Validation is external, but self-worth stems from within. For many of my clients, they lacked self-worth or the ability to feel a sense of pride in their accomplishments. My work allowed me to move them from a place in which they sought external validation to a place where they were able to increase their self-worth to take ownership and pride in how they felt about themselves.

Chief Emotional Themes

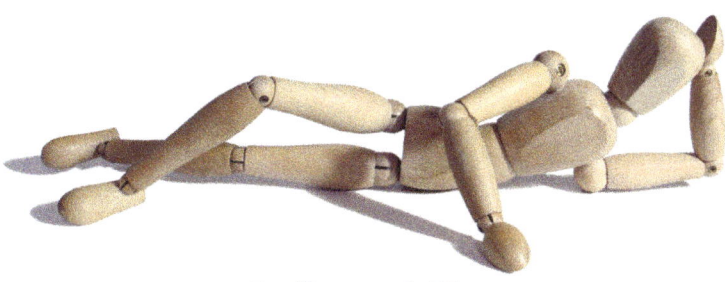

4. Inflated Ego

There's a saying that suggests pride comes before the fall. This was another theme that was prevalent in many clients. Some of them adopted a god-complex and believed they were bigger and badder than they actually were. Interestingly, while this may appear to be the opposite of the self-worth issue, it can actually originate from the same fundamental problem. Clients who exuded inflated self-worth often struggled with feelings of inferiority, but this only came to light after a period of intense probing and honest self-reflection.

5. Abandonment

It was an unfortunate circumstance, but another common source of neurosis for many of my clients stemmed from abandonment issues. Whether they'd been forsaken by parents, guardians, or caretakers at a young age, or by romantic partners later on in life, for some individuals, the feeling of abandonment pervaded their emotional experiences and colored the lens with which they interpreted the world. As a result, they were unable to move forward into new or existing relationships for fear that the other party would leave. Abandonment issues could also come from death, or the sense that a loved one "left" before the person had a chance to make things right or say goodbye.

Author Questions

1. What part of the biopsychosocial model do these themes fall under?

2. Can you think of any other themes that might fall under different parts of the model?

3. What chief emotional themes rule your character's expressions?

In no way do these categories represent a comprehensive list of where people might fall on the emotional or clinical spectrum, but in sum, I realized when I was able to drill down to the root cause of my clients' problems, they seemed to emanate from any one of these foundational issues.

We all know that everyone is different and not everyone will fit neatly into these four categories—after all, these are simply my observations based on personal experience with clients in my town; and if you have more than one child, you should be able to corroborate this assertion with vigor. Despite this, there are critical needs, wants, and desires that everyone has, and when we think about our characters—the *real people* we create—I believe this is where we should begin

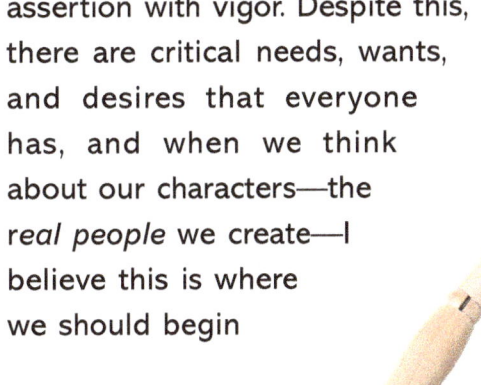

the process, by understanding who they are at the core.

How Does This Relate?

When thinking about your characters, question how these five emotional themes (or more if you can come up with some) relate to their circumstances in the story.

1. Has unconditional positive regard been an issue for them?

2. Are they constantly being judged by friends and family?

3. Does your character need validation from others?

4. How do these circumstances affect their self-esteem and ego?

It may be the case that your character falls under more than one theme, and perhaps *all* of them are relevant. In clinical terms, this is called comorbidity and it happens when a client presents with multiple diagnoses (think schizophrenia along with substance abuse/dependence). This can make for a very complex character while writing your book, but there's also the possibility that your character would have *too* much going on. Imagine a character who has low self-esteem, ADHD, and agoraphobia (fear of being in public places). How in the world would you get all these characteristics onto the page in a way that enhances the character, as opposed to detracting from them?

I'm not suggesting it's impossible, but it might be simpler to limit it to one or two of your character's traumas and let those dominate the story. As the author, you'll need to figure out which chief emotional theme will govern your character's behavior. The chief emotional theme is the trauma that trumps all the others. This is the one that shows up in the story and has the most dramatic impact on the story and character arcs.

> *Tip*
> See the chief emotional themes worksheet in the Psychological Tools section to identify your character's emotional theme(s) as well as their chief emotional theme.

Chief Emotional Themes

CHAPTER RECAP

1. There are at least five emotional themes that psychological issues fall under.
   - **Unconditional Positive Regard**: a clinical term that means, "No matter what you do, I'm not gonna stop loving you."
   - **Validation**: when someone feels they can never do anything right. Lack of positive reinforcement from significant others.
   - **Self-Worth**: stems from within. Inability to feel a sense of pride in their accomplishments.
   - **Inflated Ego**: a god-complex, believing you are bigger and badder than you actually are.
   - **Abandonment:** When someone has been forsaken by parents, guardians, or caretakers at a young age, or by romantic partners later on in life.

2. Use these themes to assist in the process of uncovering your character's *root issues*.

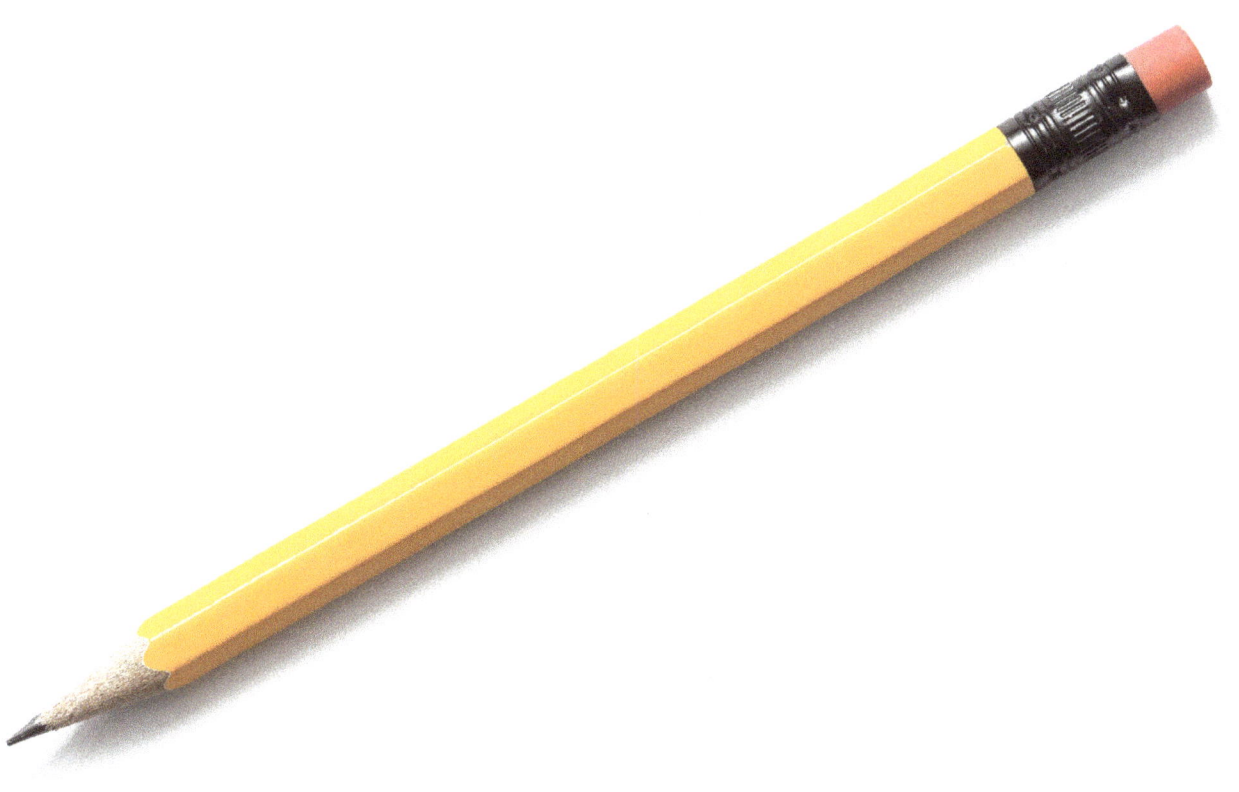

Chapter 7

PSYCHOLOGY 101

s a reminder, I'm suggesting that we know our characters.

Like, *really* know them.

This means we need to get to the nitty-gritty of who they are and why they are the way they are.

Consider my drug-addicted client, the one I referenced earlier. Unless he was born to an addicted mother, he didn't *start* life as a drug addict (think bio). And even then, if he was under the care of qualified and attentive medical staff, he would have been slowly weaned off the drug before he left the hospital.

Still, his unfortunate exposure to mind-altering substances in-utero potentially predisposed him to certain thoughts, mindsets, and behaviors through childhood, adolescence, and maybe even into adulthood (think psycho). As a direct consequence, this predisposition might influence how he interacts with his parents, his siblings, his teachers, his wife, and his children (think social).

Author Questions

1. To what has your character been predisposed?

2. Take it a step further: how does this show up in your story?

If we're regarding our characters as real people (which we absolutely should be), we need to carefully consider the ways in which this predisposition will impact their behavior within the pages of our story.

This is the foundation of 3D character design!

By understanding our characters' historical traumas, we are better able to craft them in compelling ways in our stories. To do this, we need to get into their minds, but our inquiry must be deliberate and intentional.

What follows are some psychological theories I have personally used to better understand my characters' behavior.

NB: This is not a comprehensive psychology study. Remember, it took me a total of seven years to get my bachelor's and master's degrees, and I spent another three years doing my PhD.

(A Few) Theories of Psychology

There are so many psychological camps and theories that to name them all here would not be productive for what we came to do. However, I am confident that each of these ideas has the potential to significantly impact the ways in which we approach character design, so if you want to switch your major, or even read a textbook on the subject, I invite you to do so.

Psychology is fascinating!

That said, to move us forward in the task of designing our 3D characters, I want to expose you, the creator of future real people, to seven psychological camps and principles that will help you consider your character's life *before* your story began.

Yes, before.

We're writing about their present circumstances. If we've done a prologue, we may have touched on their historical data, and if we do an epilogue, we may delve into what happens after we write *The End*.

Think of this as the prologue *before* the prologue, the stuff that happened to your character before page 1.

Why is this important?

Because if we're going to successfully design 3D characters who demand five-star reviews like the ones I've been fortunate enough to get under my pen name, it's not enough to simply know them at the moment their story begins.

We want to be present at their births.

We need to watch them grow up.

We must see how they handled the bully on the playground in grade school and experienced their first kiss in high school.

We need to know what makes them happy and what they're afraid of.

Understanding the theories of psychology for real people will help us achieve this objective. By meeting our characters *before* the story begins, we'll have a deep understanding of who they really are and how they came to be, which will make them jump off the page.

Psychology works.

I'm a huge proponent of the field because I have seen the way good therapy changes the trajectory of people's lives, and when we begin to think of our characters as real, living, breathing individuals, we can apply these fact-finding techniques to their design and to our stories.

Even though there are tons of psychological principles, I believe the ones I'm about to highlight will be sufficient for us to begin the exciting task of crafting 3D characters who will resonate with our readers. This is the way in which I approach character design, and my hope is that you will take this into consideration as you design yours.

As you read the following information, actively consider your character and the ways in which these concepts might be applicable. Don't worry; I'll provide examples and questions to jolt your thinking, and when you facilitate your "therapy session" with the character, you'll get a chance to delve even deeper.

1. Psychoanalysis

Perhaps you've heard of the man many deem to be the father of psychology, Sigmund Freud. There is so much that can be said about this groundbreaking pioneer, but for the purposes of this book, the only thing we need to know is that he believed humans operated according to *subconscious influences*.[3]

What in the world does that mean?

Freud was of the opinion that angst, turmoil, and internal struggle are the results of thoughts, feelings, and emotions happening beneath the surface of the mind. (Examples: the cigarette your character smokes? Their mother weaned them off the breast too early. That obsessive-compulsive thing your neighbor has going on? They got stuck in the anal stage of their development.)

Freud was the guy with the couch, the one you see in the movies and may have even included in one or two of your stories. Clients are encouraged to lie on his magical sofa and explore their subconscious thoughts, which, he purported, influenced conscious behavior.

Freud also talked about the **Id**, the **Ego,** and the **Superego.**[4] The *Id* is the insatiable part of us, the one that wants what it wants and now! The *Ego* is the practical version of the Id. This is the subconscious part that acknowledges the Id's desire, but reasons with it to suggest that it should be strategic about how to obtain it. The *Superego* is the moral part of the human subconscious. This part acknowledges the desire and accepts there is a time and place for it but goes further to question the morality of it.

This approach stresses that mental health problems are rooted in unconscious conflicts and desires. In order to resolve the mental angst, these undercover struggles must be identified and addressed. Psychoanalysis often does this through exploring one's early childhood experiences that may have continuing repercussions

---

[4] Freud reference: Kupfersmid, J. (2019). Freud's Clinical Theories Then and Now. Psychodynamic Psychiatry, 47(1), 81-97.

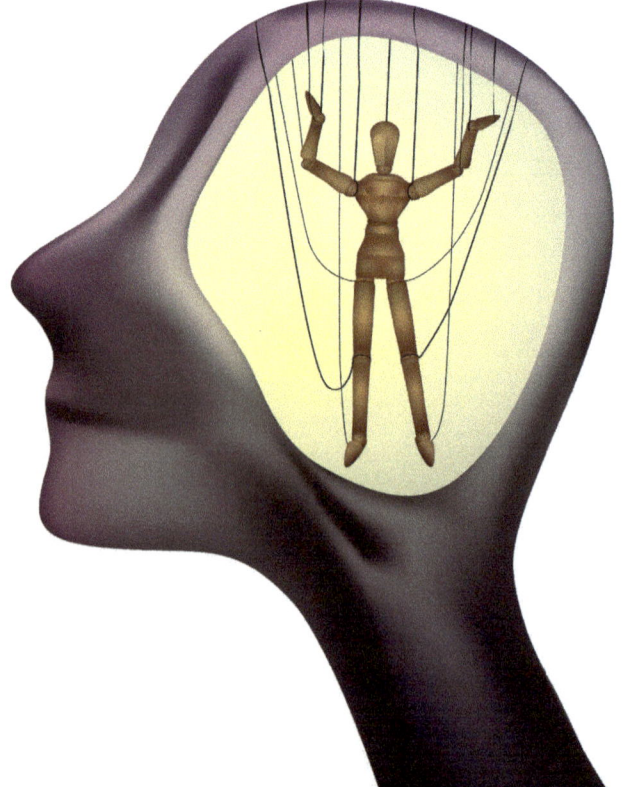

---

[3] (Clark, 2010) (Kupfersmid., 2019)

on one's mental health in the present and later in life.

> *Author Questions*
>
> 1. Does your character operate primarily with his **Id**, **Ego**, or **Superego**? How do you know this?
>
> 2. What subconscious beliefs does your character have about the world that influence their behavior?
>
> 3. Under the premise of psychoanalysis, what does your character's arc look like over the course of your story?

> ***Tip***
>
> See the character development interview chart in the Psychological Tools section.

2. Cognitive Behavioral Psychology

Cognitive behavioral psychology[5] is a combination of behavioral psychology (which focuses on changing behavior using systematic processes, like pairing consequences with behavior—think punishment and reward) and cognitive psychology (which focuses on changing the thoughts and beliefs a person has, with the ultimate goal of changing how they behave).

Regarding punishment and reward, this is like the karmic principle or the saying, "you reap what you sow." Our characters will make decisions over the course of our stories, and they will be the beneficiaries of the natural consequences that come along with those choices.

The ABC Principle

Cognitive behavioral therapy also uses the **ABC principle**,[6] where A is the antecedent (or the inciting incident—the trigger event), *B* is the belief people attach to the inciting incident, and *C* is the consequence or resulting action the person takes based on the belief they've adopted about the inciting incident.

This approach focuses on changing the way a client thinks about a situation (the automatic thoughts they immediately associate with a trigger or event), with a view to alter their emotional or behavioral response to it. For example, a client who notices that their significant other isn't talking to them may assume they have done something wrong, or think the relationship is in jeopardy. However, those who have experience with cognitive behavioral therapy would challenge the "B" (belief of the inciting incident) and seek to modify the client's thoughts about the "C" (consequence about the belief), which would potentially reduce their anxiety or change the resulting behavior. To clarify this principle, let's use the above client who is anxious because their significant other isn't communicating. Using the ABC framework, that client might be encouraged to consider that their significant other isn't talking to them because they aren't feeling well

---

[5] CBT Reference: Clark, V. (2010). CBT for Beginners. Drug and Alcohol Review, 29(2),

[6] ABC Reference: Ellis, A. (2005). The revised ABC's of rational-emotive therapy (RET). Journal of Rational-Emotive & Cognitive-Behavior Therapy, 9(3), 139-172.

(not because they're angry). If the client accepts this as a plausible option, they're anxiety might be reduced and they might seek other ways to approach the situation.

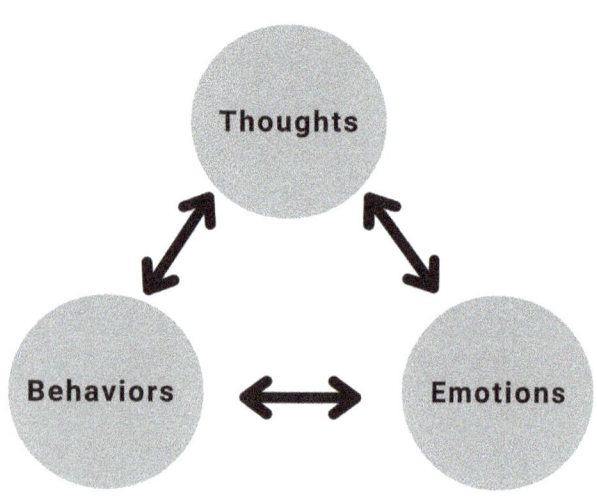

The Cognitive Triangle shows how thoughts, behaviors and emotions affect one another.

In the graphic, the situation triggers a thought, which elicits emotion and then produces behavior, which then reinforces the thought. The therapist's job is to help the client create a new thought about the situation, which will presumably influence the remainder of the cycle. Similarly, the author's job is to help the character create a new thought (using the story and character arcs) about the situation, which will undoubtedly influence the remainder of the story.

Author Questions

1. What is the *ABC* for my character? What is happening to them (A)? What do they believe about what's happening (B)? How do they behave based on what they believe (C)?

2. Think about the behavior part of cognitive behavioral therapy (CBT). What punishment or reward does your character experience based on their actions?

3. What is a consequence your character will experience as a result of their behavior in your story?

4. Under the premise of CBT, what does your character's arc look like over the course of your story?

Tip
See the blank CBT-related forms in the Psychological Tools section.

3. Developmental Psychology

Developmental psychology is concerned with *"the way people evolve over the course of their lifespan and considers how thinking, feeling, and behavior change over time."*[7] For example, a child and an adult might be exposed to the

---

[7] (Masters, 1981).

same situation but based on their developmental stage and the development of their brains, they will experience it differently.

Regarding our characters, the way they thought when they were children is different than the way they think about things as adults.

One of the big ideas coming out of developmental psychology is the **nature versus nurture**[8] debate. Specifically, is development more affected by biology and genetic makeup, or is environment the most influential factor?

Author Questions

1. Here's a hypothetical situation: an item of value goes missing. How would your character interpret this during childhood (three years old)? How might they interpret it in early adulthood (twenty-three years old)? Later adulthood (seventy-three years old)?

2. Think of your character's personality. Are they the way they are because their parents were that way *(nature)*? Or did their home environment cause them to be that way *(nurture)*?

3. Under the premise of developmental psychology, what does your character's arc look like over the course of your story?

---

[8] Nature/nurture reference: Eagly, A., & Wood, W. (2013). The Nature–Nurture Debates. Perspectives on Psychological Science, 8(3), 340-357.

4. Attachment Theory (Developmental Psychology)

In developmental psychology, "attachment theory" investigates *the emotional bond between one human and another and how this influences their emotional and mental health.*[9] This theory suggests that a caregiver/mother must exhibit adequate nurturing to their newborn to establish a close bond. If this is not done, it can lead to several emotional problems later on in life for the child into adulthood.

Author Questions

1. Did your character have a good relationship with their parents? Based on your answer, how does this impact their relationship with their significant other and other characters in the story?

2. Under the premise of developmental psychology, what does your character's arc look like over the course of your story?

---

[9] Bolen (Lester, 2013), R. (2000). Validity of Attachment Theory. Trauma, Violence, & Abuse, 1(2), 128-153.

5. Maslow's Hierarchy of Needs (Developmental Psychology)

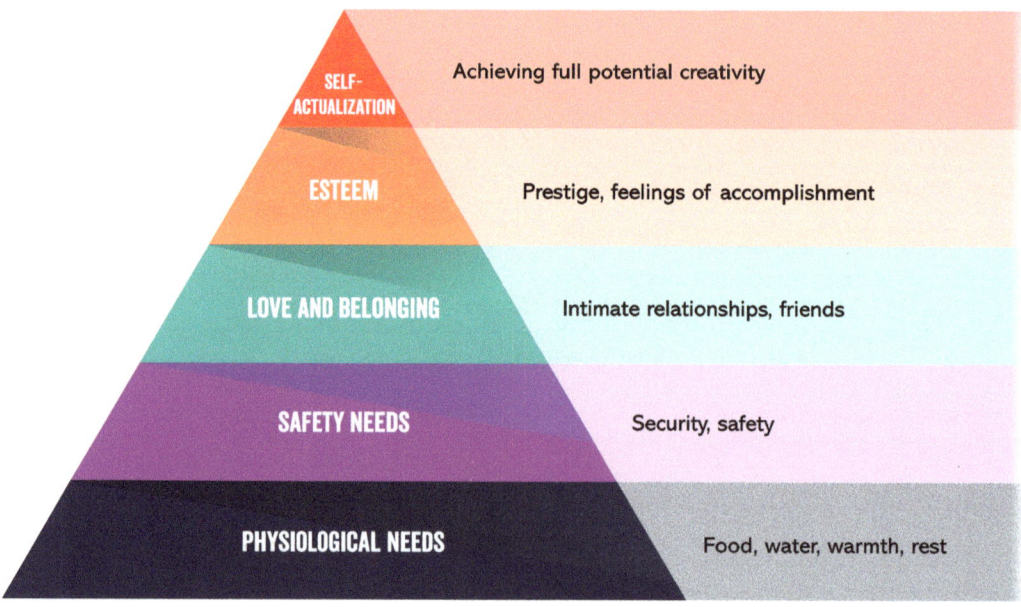

Abraham Maslow[10] was a developmental psychologist who believed that *for people to reach self-actualization at the top of the above pyramid, they had to successfully make their way through (and conquer) each of the tiers below it.* If a person becomes stuck on any one of these tiers, they will experience emotional distress and even trauma, which will prevent them from becoming fully self-actualized adults. According to Maslow, this is the root of psychological un-wellness.

Author Questions

1. Is your character stuck on any of the tiers? How do you know?
2. What might this look like in your story? How will it play out?
3. Under the premise of Maslow's Hierarchy of Needs, what does your character's arc look like over the course of your story?

Tip
See the blank Maslow's Hierarchy of Needs chart in the Psychological Tools section.

---

[10] Maslow reference: Lester, D. (2013). Measuring Maslow's Hierarchy of Needs. Psychological Reports, 113(1), 15-17.

Psychology 101

6. Person-Centered Therapy (PCT)

Person-centered therapy[11] suggests *emotional distress is the result of an inconsistency between the client's behavior and their true personal identity*. With person-centered therapy, the therapist's goal is to create an environment in which clients can discover their self-worth, explore their identities, and alter their behavior to better reflect it. If a client (or your character) is unable to reconcile this, they will be emotionally impaired.

Author Questions

1. How does your character behave in your story? What is their personality like?
2. Is this consistent with their true identity? How do you know?
3. Under the premise of person-centered therapy, what does their character's arc look like over the course of your story?

7. Johari Window

	Known to Self	Unknown to self
Known to others	**Open Self** — Information about you that both you & others know	**Blind Self** — Information about you that you don't know but others do
Unknown to Others	**Hidden Self** — Information about you that you know but others don't	**Unknown Self** — Information about you that neither you nor others know

The Johari Window[12] is a method that was designed to help people understand their relationship with themselves and others.

The **Open Self** is the part everyone sees and knows, even your character.

The **Blind Self** is the part others see, but your character does not.

The **Hidden Self** is the part your character knows about himself, but of which others are unaware.

Finally, the **Unknown Self** is that part no one knows about—not even the character.

---

[11] Narknisorn, B. (2012). Person-Centered Therapy and Personal Growth. *Journal of Social and Development Sciences*

[12] Berland, A. (2017). Using the Johari Window to explore patient and provider perspectives. *International Journal of Health Governance, 22*(1), 47-51.

The goal of this strategy is to help the client become aware of each of the four quadrants, so they can better understand their thoughts, feelings, and behaviors.

Author Questions

1. What does your character's **Open Self** look like? How does this play out in your story?
2. What does your character's **Blind Self** look like? How does this play out in your story?
3. What does your character's **Hidden Self** look like? How does this play out in your story?
4. What does your character's **Unknown Self** look like? How does this play out in your story?
5. Under the premise of the Johari Window, what does your character's arc look like over the course of your story?

Tip
See the blank Johari Window chart in the Psychological Tools section.

CHAPTER RECAP

1. Psychoanalysis: humans operate according to subconscious influences.

2. The Id is the insatiable part of us.

3. The Ego is the practical version of the Id.

4. The Superego is the moral part of the human subconscious.

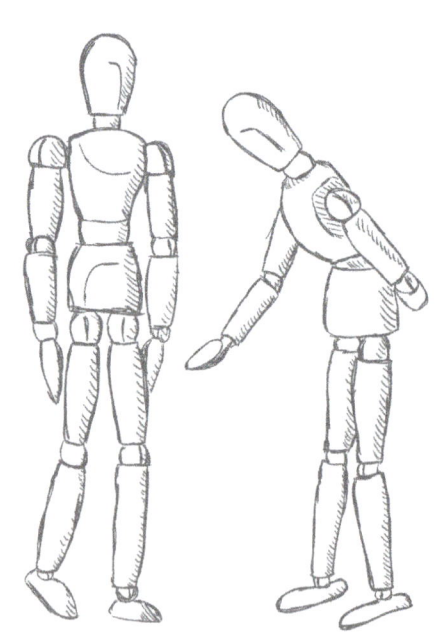

5. Cognitive-behavioral Psychology: a combination of behavioral psychology and cognitive psychology.

6. ABC principle: A = antecedent; B = belief; C = consequence

7. Developmental Psychology: the way people evolve over the course of their lifespan.

8. Nature versus Nurture: is development more affected by biology or environment?

9. Attachment Theory: the emotional bond between humans.

10. Maslow's Hierarchy of Needs: self-actualization comes when people successfully conquer prior developmental milestones.

11. Person-Centered Therapy: emotional distress is the result of an inconsistency between the person's behavior and their true, personal identity.

12. Johari Window: Open Self (the part everyone sees and knows); Blind Self (the part others see, but your character does not); Hidden Self (the part your character knows about himself, but of which others are unaware); Unknown Self (the part no one knows about—not even the character).

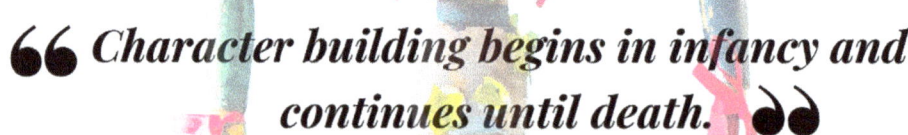

" *Character building begins in infancy and continues until death.* "

ELEANOR ROOSEVELT

Chapter 8

APPLYING PSYCHOLOGICAL THEORY TO CHARACTER DESIGN

Applying Psychology to Character Development

Character Therapy Sessions

Did you survive the crash course? If you did, you're now armed with a basic understanding of a few psychological theories and their assumptions about how people come to be who they are in the present. And if you answered the Author Questions, you are beginning to get ideas about who your character is beyond what they tell you (think Blind Self).

Now that we have these tools, we're going to use them to get up close and personal with our characters to conduct a therapy session with them!

> **NB**: Once you have worked through these processes a couple of times, you will find it easier to interview your character **prior to** application of the psychological tools.

Earlier, I said the heart of a story is the character. I still believe this, but now I'd like to expand on this and suggest that the other heart of the story are the character's problems.

We all have problems. In fact, Henry Ford once said, "there are no big problems, just a lot of little ones[13]." With this in mind, our characters come to us with a dilemma we need to help them solve. They are depending on us to help them steer through the character and story arcs so when we get to "The End," they would have found some semblance of a happily ever after. (And if you're writing romance like I do, you'd better have one of those.)

Equipped with this conviction, when I talk to my characters, I'm *actively* listening to what they say. I watch their nonverbal cues and take

---

[13] www.brainyquotes.com

Applying Psychological Theory To Character Design

notes about the ways in which it all adds up. Because I'm a people-watcher, I'm desperate to know what caused them to arrive at their current states, assume their archetypes, and understand the ways in which their pasts and presents relate (deliberate application of psychological principles). Specifically, I'm curious about why they got married and divorced. I want to know their triggers and the things that set them on edge. I also want to know about the things that make them smile.

All these nuances help me make predictions about what my characters are going to do and why they are going to do it. This information also helps me to think of potential barriers to success and solutions (think plot). The key is taking the time to know the characters from the inside out.

Sometimes the information will automatically come to you. Your character's personality will be so strong and vibrant you'll be able to read them. . .like a book. For example, when my extremely alpha hero Andrés Reinoso from my popular *El Rey* series whispered in my ear and told me I needed to write his story, his personality slammed me against the wall. I could see him standing there, accomplished and brave, but I could also detect the fear beneath his posture, which alerted me that despite his initial presentation into my subconscious, all was not well (think Hidden Self).

Other times, depending on your character's backstory, you may have to poke and prod to find out what they are really about. This was the case with my wolf-shifter hero, Remi Moretti in my novel *Torn*. He was strong and brave, but he was so layered, it took a while for me to discover he had abandonment issues (think Unknown Self).

Your characters may not reveal themselves to you right away. Think about it; people *never* tell therapists the whole truth in the first therapy session, but it's your job as the author to dig through the rubble of your character's trauma and uncover the pearls that will make for a satisfactory character arc. This is the thing that connects readers to your characters and, ultimately, the story. To do this, we need to understand each thread, which comprises the tapestry of our beautiful characters.

You are now ready to conduct your first therapy session with the 3D characters you're creating! Your overall mission will be to authentically represent your character in your story. Now, we're going to talk to them to determine exactly what the real issues are.

NB: This is a very intense free-writing exercise, and the objective is to see and feel your characters at their core. Earlier, I said that the story is not about you; I'm saying it again here. To develop 3D characters, it is imperative that you step outside of yourself and give your characters the space and freedom to manifest before your very eyes.

When conducting therapy sessions with your characters, the key is to let your imagination go. For this therapy session to work, allow yourself to imagine freely and without distractions.

But how do you do that?

The truth is, this may be easier for some authors to do more than others and is partially dependent on which side of the brain you're wired to engage. In other words, some of us are naturally left-brained thinkers[14] (analytical and methodical), where others of us (myself included) are more prone to right-brain thinking[15] activity (creative and artistic).

To be clear, no one is better than the other. In fact, it is entirely possible to balance the two operations and apply them to particular situations; however, if you primarily identify as a right-brainer, this exercise will be right up your alley! You probably talk to your characters all the time. Not only that, but you probably see them as well. These are right-brain responses to the art of crafting stories, and you're most likely excited about what's to come.

However, if you're a left-brainer, you may find it difficult to engage in such an illogical task. *How in the world are you supposed to talk to people that don't even exist? And how in the world are you supposed to hear them when they answer your questions?* These are left-brain questions that probably popped into your mind the minute you reached this chapter. But don't let these reservations deter you.

If you find it difficult to engage in the following highly creative exercise, try applying these tips:

Left-Brain/Right-Brain Conversion Tips

1. Release any preconceived notions of logic (just for a moment), which will only hamper your creative self, as well as developing your characters.

2. Find a quiet area, free from distractions, which will allow you to fully engage in the creative exercise and relax.

3. Use any notes you've written about your characters to enhance your ability to actually visualize them. What are they wearing? What are their facial expressions? What does their voice sound like? Allow these "facts" to materialize in your imagination.

4. Don't judge yourself (or your characters). You're not crazy. You're creative.

---

[14] (Corballis, 2014)

[15] (Corballis 2014)

Brain Waves and Creativity

I don't believe in writers' block; however, no author will deny that there are times when your story gets stuck (especially if you're a panster, one who writes without an outline). You write your characters into a corner, and they become oppositional. They refuse to do what you and the plot want them to, and the next thing you know, your manuscript is driving you up a wall.

As a panster, I've run into this problem more times than I'd like to admit, and when I quit my job to write full time, I quickly realized that I needed to find a reliable solution—and fast! Indeed, there are many books, blog posts, and YouTube videos that address this frustrating topic, but when I was forced to shut down my laptop and engage in an activity that had nothing to do with the story (such as going to sleep), I stumbled upon something almost magical. Suddenly, just before lapsing into a deep slumber, the once elusive solution to my story-problem would reveal itself. It didn't just happen once, either. Pretty consistently, I'd find resolutions to the issues in my story, jump out of bed, and begin writing again.

What in the world was happening?

I simply had to know.

My research led me to the phenomenon of brain wave activity and the idea that there is a particular mode that appears to be the breeding ground for creativity. According to researchers,[16] there are four types of brain waves: beta, alpha, theta, and delta. To describe each, your brain operates in *beta* when your conscious mind is focused and driven by what you need to do. For example, when I'm teaching my writing workshops or engaging in one-on-one coaching with an aspiring author, I'm in full beta mode.

Once I've successfully completed these tasks, my brain moves into *alpha* mode. I'm suddenly relaxed, as I shut down my computer and take Beau, my Pomsky, for a rejuvenating walk on the beach.

As we're sauntering along the pink Bermuda sand, my brain will automatically shift into *theta*. This happens because walking on the beach is a mindless task, which doesn't require much cognitive manpower. This mode also appears when I'm doing cardio on the treadmill or (get this) just before I fall asleep or wake up.

Finally, my brain shifts to *delta* just before I fall into a deep sleep and is the time when the rapid eye movement (REM) stage of sleep occurs.

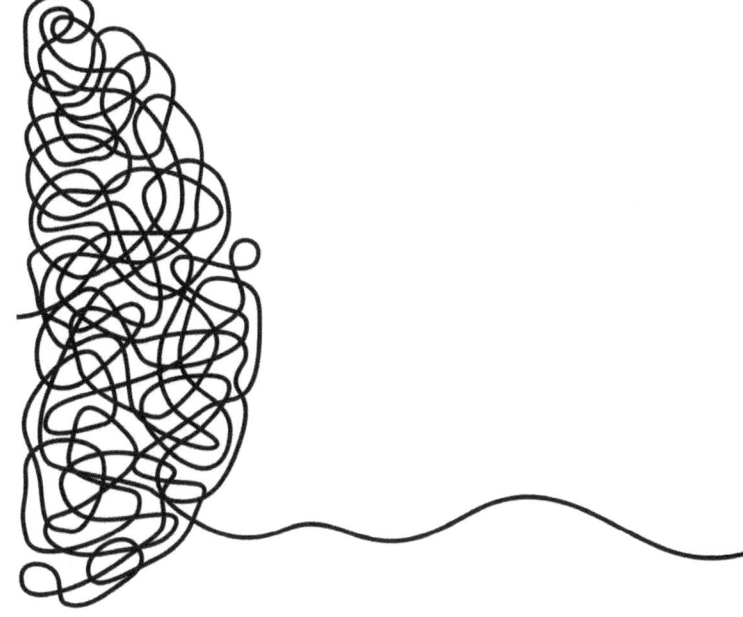

More About Theta

What I came to realize, first through experience and then through research, was that just before I fell asleep, my characters would suddenly come to life and the obstacle I'd been

---

[16] Boynton, T. (2001). Applied Research Using Alpha/Theta Training for Enhancing Creativity and Well-Being. Journal of Neurotherapy.

knocking my head against for hours suddenly vanished. The more it happened, the more I'd deliberately "go to sleep," and while I was "sleeping," I'd intentionally think about my story, consistently come up with an innovative remedy, jump out of bed, and resume the task of writing.

And I'm not the only creative to experience this.

Reportedly, chemist Kekule claimed to discover benzene during this stage,[17] and Mozart created many a masterpiece while in this state. He's quoted as saying:

> When I am, as it were, completely myself, entirely alone, and of good cheer-say, traveling in a carriage, or walking after a good meal, or during the night when I cannot sleep; it is on such occasions that my ideas flow best and most abundantly. Whence and how they come, I do not know; nor can I force them.... All this fires my soul, and, provided that I am not disturbed, my subject enlarges itself, becomes methodized and defined, and the whole, though it be long, stands almost complete and finished in my mind, so that I can survey it, like a fine picture or a beautiful statue, at a glance. Nor do I hear in my imagination the parts successively, but I hear them, as it were, all at once. What a delight this is I cannot tell! All this inventing, this producing, takes place in a pleasing lively dream.

Boynton explains that this level of brain wave activity has been known to have several names, including *hypnagogia, the reverie state,* and *the twilight state.*[18] Back in the 1970s, Green and colleagues conducted research that demonstrated a clear correlation between theta training and creativity. Specifically, after conducting research with participants required to manipulate alpha and theta brain waves using an EEG machine, it was determined that theta was profoundly associated with "a quieting of the body, emotions, and thoughts, thus allowing usually 'unheard things' to come to consciousness."

There was my answer! Theta (specifically the window between sleep/awake or vice versa) is where the creative magic happens.

How Does This Apply?

When I discuss writers' block with my students and clients, I often tell them "go to sleep... but not really." In other words, deliberately attempt to harness the power of theta when crafting stories and creating 3D characters. In the session you're about to have with your characters, allow your brain to lapse into theta. Stop thinking about your to-do list or the big project you've yet to tackle for your boss, and let your brain operate on rote—the mode it goes into when you're driving a familiar route or when you're engaging in some routine task, like on the treadmill or falling asleep.

Now, take it a step further.

Conduct your character therapy during these times. Just as your head hits the pillow, or when you're ten minutes into your cardio session on the treadmill, ask your character questions about who they are and why they're the way they are

---

[17] Boynton, 2008.

[18] Boynton, T., &, (2001). Applied Research Using Alpha/Theta Training for Enhancing Creativity and Well-Being. Journal of Neurotherapy

(character interview example coming up). Practice deliberately shifting your brain into theta, and watch the magic happen. Find a quiet space and relax. Release any preconceived thoughts you may have had about the exercise and let your imagination run wild. Listen carefully and allow your characters to breathe. They'll tell you the truth; you simply have to be patient with them and yourself.

Author Note

There are YouTube videos of theta music, which assists with shifting you into theta. Check out videos by Meditational State or MusicMindMagic to get started.

Let's get started by using three of my alpha men Patrick, Maverick, and Rey (from my books Pied, Five Years, and Reinoso), and see what gems we can uncover.

> **NB**: *The therapy sessions you're about to read do not represent a full-length session. In real life, I would have continued until my characters stopped talking. Don't stop until your imagination goes quiet!*

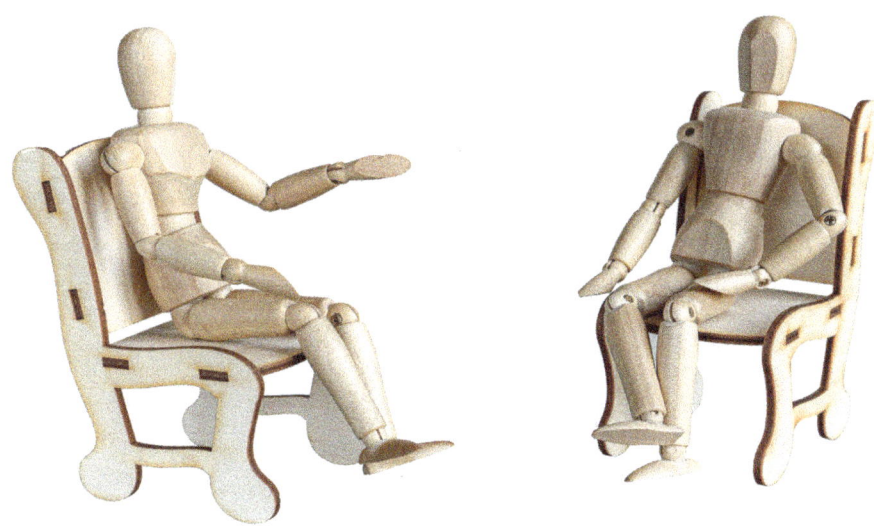

The Psychology of Character Building for Authors

SESSION 1

Maverick Dangerfield

"5 Years"

Author: Mav, what has brought you in today?
Maverick: My boss says I have anger issues, but I have no idea what he's talking about.
Author: Tell me more about that.
Maverick: The other day, an underling got on my nerves, and I fired his ass on the spot.
Author: Underling…?
Maverick: That's what he is! He's beneath me. He's incompetent and useless. I fired him, and I'll find someone else who can do the job the way I want it done.
Author: I notice your posture.
Maverick: What do you mean?
Author: You're tense. You're grimacing. Your jaw is ticking.
Maverick: *(Silence)*
Author: I wonder what emotion you're feeling right now.
Maverick: I'm pissed as fuck!
Author: Tell me more.
Maverick: My boss sent me here as if something is wrong with me, but I'm not the one with the problem!
Author: *(As the author, I notice that Maverick is more tense. Now his nostrils are flaring.)* You definitely appear angry right now, but I wonder if there's something underneath the anger. Anger is normally a byproduct of a more primal emotion, like sadness. What are you really feeling?
Maverick: *(Pauses.)* I guess I feel a little worthless, like I'm not good enough. My mom used to say those things to me.
Author: That must have been hurtful.
Maverick: Yeah, it was.
…

Applying Psychological Theory To Character Design

SESSION 2

Patrick "The Pied" Piper

"Pied"

Author: Pat, what has brought you in today?
Patrick: My name is Patrick.
Author: I apologize.
Patrick: And I don't really need to be here. There is nothing wrong with me.
Author: You look very successful. I can see why you'd say that, but if I'm going to write your story, something must be up. There must be some issue.
Patrick: There's no issue. There's a woman I want and the moment I meet her, I will have her.
Author: You seem sure of yourself.
Patrick: Certainly. I always get what I want. This will be no different.
Author: Has there ever been a time when you've not gotten what you wanted?
Patrick: *(Pauses.)* Maybe when I was a little boy, but that was a long time ago.
Author: So, you forget what happened?
Patrick: No, but I'd rather not talk about it.
Author: *(Noticing posture—his expression is tightening, and his body is turning rigid.)* It must be a painful memory.
Patrick: I beg your pardon?
Author: I mean, there must be some reason why you don't want to talk about it. I guess I'm assuming that it's not pleasant.
Patrick: Look, my parents weren't the best parents in the world. They wouldn't have won any awards.
Author: Tell me about your childhood, Patrick. What is your earliest memory?
…

SESSION 3

Andrés Reinoso

"Reinoso—El Rey Series, Book 1"

Author: Rey, what has brought you in today?
Rey: *(Chest pokes out)* Me gusta una mujer y…
Author: I'm sorry to cut you off, but my Spanish is a little rusty.
Rey: Oh. Right. I was saying, there's a woman who's come into my life, and I think I'm falling for her, but there's too much shit going on in the streets and I don't have time for love.
Author: I get that. You're a busy man, but when you say you don't have time for love…
Rey: It's a distraction. I run an empire, and it can be dangerous out there. I've got enemies. If anything happened to her, I'd never forgive myself. I've already lost people I care about.
Author: That must have been tough. In fact, I can tell from the look on your face that there's still a lot of pain.
Rey: *(Jaw clenches)*
Author: So, you don't have time for love.
Rey: No.
Author: Has it always been like that?
…

Applying Psychological Theory To Character Design

The therapy sessions you just read were not rehearsed, prewritten, or re-drafted. I literally began to type the things I heard my characters say and saw them do. That said, part of the refining process might require me to go back in and do some tweaking.

Notice the *italicized* portions. This was the moment I saw my characters as they were—I witnessed their behavior, nonverbal cues, and body language. This was exciting because it gave me a glimpse into the character's Hidden Self. Despite their "words," I was able to draw conclusions about their real motivations and desires, because of my understanding of psychological principles. As a result, I was also able to get a clearer understanding of their lives, conflicts, and the ways in which it could potentially play out in their stories.

Also, notice the way certain words my characters used in this free-write therapy session stood out to me. Maverick called his employee an "underling." To me, this suggested superiority that he looks down on people and perhaps has a sense of entitlement (**Emotional Theme:** Ego). I immediately questioned how this might play out in my story in the form of dialogue and narrative. It also caused me to wonder about the origin of this mindset and which psychological theory was applicable.

It would now be my job to get this onto the page and authentically represent my character.

Then there was Patrick, who corrected me when I called him "Pat." I could see him sitting there, entitled and pompous. I was beneath him. He was royalty. Like Maverick, Patrick also presented himself with a sense of entitlement, but his energy was a lot stronger. It seemed as if he felt the world owed him something.

Where did this come from?

I started to get an idea of the answer to this question when I asked about his relationship with his parents (**Attachment Theory**). At that point, his posture changed. He even faltered a little. I could tell I was getting somewhere, and with continued questioning, I would have uncovered the root issue as well as the *ABC* (**Cognitive Behavioral Therapy**).

Rey started off his session speaking in his native language. This told me that he was very proud of his Latino heritage, as he should be (**Person-Centered Therapy**). He was very well-dressed, flashy in fact. His national pride shone through, and as I began to write his story, it was my job to show this pride to the reader using the principles of *show, don't tell*; however, when I asked about love, some of Rey's bravado faded. In fact, when he said he didn't have time for love, it made me wonder if he'd always felt that way and what that might look like in my story.

All this information may not (and probably *should* not) make it into your final draft, but it should certainly show up in your exposition in some way, shape, or form. To be clear, this is not a call to info-dump or bombard your reader with mundane, irrelevant facts about the character's backstory; rather, the objective is to allow the information to color your character's responses and enrich the reader's experience.

Tips For Conducting Your Therapy Session

When you are conducting your free-write therapy session, allow your natural curiosity to take control. I'm a people-watcher so this comes naturally to me, but if you see your characters as *real* people, this will be easy for you as well. It may be difficult at first, but the more you do it, the easier it will become.

Because this is a free-write exercise, it would be counterproductive to prescribe how it should go, but here are some points to keep in mind as you engage your character and your imagination:

1. **Notice** your character's nonverbal cues and make mention of them.

2. **Listen** for keywords. Bring them up and see what your character's response is.

3. **Ask** your character open-ended, probing questions, not closed-ended ones, which will only elicit yes/no responses.

4. **Ask** your character about their childhood and their relationships with parental figures and siblings. Consider using these age ranges: 0-2 years, 3-12 years, 13-18 years, young adulthood, middle adulthood, and old age.

5. **Let your character talk.** Listen quietly and understand that the first thing you hear is the accurate response. This isn't about deleting or erasing; it's about flow and feeling.

6. **Role Play.** This is a technique therapists use in sessions, and this is essentially what I'm encouraging you to do here. I want you to really think of yourself as a therapist and really think of your character as your client. Also, consider using a friend or family member who can act as your client/character and respond to your questions and prompts; this will work best if they have a deep understanding of the character, or if they have similar personalities.

7. **Think like your character.** You may not be a billionaire business mogul (Maverick) or a Latino, street king (Rey). Heck, you may not even be the Pied Piper of Hamelin (Patrick), but step into your character's shoes and try to *be* them for a few minutes.

8. **Don't stop exploring** until your character (read: imagination) does. The more your character talks, the more questions you'll have.

I'VE GOT THE GEMS. NOW WHAT?

We're now equipped with rich information about our characters' traumatic backstories. We've conducted our first of many therapy sessions and have uncovered rich information about their subconscious and automatic thoughts, their cognitive-behavioral responses, their attachments and relationships with caregivers, their true identities, and their open, blind, hidden, and unknown selves. Not only that, but we've identified the archetypes and have a working awareness of their strengths and weaknesses.

As we begin to pull it all together, we need to make connections between what we've learned and what they said.

Don't worry if this seems daunting. I promise, the more you engage in this process, the easier it will become.

Applying Psychological Theory To Character Design

Let's use Patrick as an example of how we might pull this information together:

Psychological Application Form

Theory: **Attachment Theory**
Character Name: **Patrick 'Pied' Piper**

Keywords:	Open, Blind, Hidden, Unknown Self
	Quick Notes
1.	Clearly has a poor attachment style with his parents, especially his father. This impacts his relationship with other characters in the book, especially his love interest.

Psychological Application Form

Theory: **Johari Window**
Character Name: **Patrick 'Pied' Piper**

Keywords:	Open, Blind, Hidden, Unknown Self
	Quick Notes
1.	Character's 'Open Self' is confident, I know this because of what I 'saw' in the therapy session; however, it is obvious he's trying to keep his 'Hidden self' hidden.
2.	'Blind Self' notes: Overbearing and authoritarian which might be his way of trying to keep others away from the truth of his pain (his horrible upbringing).

 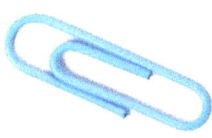

Psychological Application Form

Theory: **Cognitive Behavioral Therapy**
Character Name: **Patrick 'Pied' Piper**

Keywords:	ABC, punishment, reward, thought processes, distorted thoughts.
	Quick Notes
1.	A= Doesn't get what he wants. B = He is being disrespected. C = Lashes out on others.
2.	Punishment (because of his behavior): other characters pull away from him, including his love interest. Reward (perceived): people are intimidated by him and obey his commands.

55

Psychological Application Form

Theory: **Maslow's Hierarchy of Needs**
Character Name: **Patrick 'Pied' Piper**

Keywords:	Tiers/stages, conquer, stuck.
	Quick Notes
1.	Stuck on Tier 3 (Belongingness & love). This is due to his poor (abusive) relationship with his parents. Also due to lack of trust in adults.

Psychological Application Form

Theory: **Person-Centered Therapy**
Character Name: **Patrick 'Pied' Piper**

Keywords:	Identity, congruence, true-self, inconsistency
	Quick Notes
1.	Character isn't in touch with his true-self. He doesn't even know who he truly is. He uses prestige as a facade to mask his true issues.

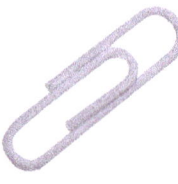

Psychological Application Form

Theory: **Psychoanalysis**
Character Name: **Patrick 'Pied' Piper**

Keywords:	Id, Ego, Superego; subconscious thoughts, desires.
	Quick Notes
1.	Controlled by his Id. This looks like him wearing his heart on his sleeve and being reactionary. Doesn't really care about others' emotions. Lacks empathy.
2.	Subconsciously he feels inferior but he doesn't know this. Maybe this ties into the concept of his hidden self.... (??)

Applying Psychological Theory To Character Design

The forms on the previous pages assist with the process of: (1) identifying the psychological principle associated with what the character "said" during their interview; (2) highlighting the keywords associated with the identified psychological theory; (3) providing a space to jot notes based on your observations.

> ***Tip***
> Use the psychological application form in the Psychological Tools Section to follow this process.

NB: If you think you can get deeper with your character by conducting another session, feel free to do this. The goal is to collect all the pearls of information from them.

Now, to complete the task of making them 3D, we need to take it a step further and *deliberately* layer their goals, motivations, and conflicts with trauma. I know it sounds dark; however, as authors, we have no choice but to do it, especially if we want to create unforgettable characters.

So, *how* do we do it?

By using the information we have gathered so far and applying it to the character's goals, motivation, and conflict.

(BACK TO) GOALS, MOTIVATION, & CONFLICT

Recall the discussion we had about GMC in Section 1. Those were external considerations, but because we're now equipped with some psychological theory, let's turn this concept inward.

To start, let's ignore the "C" for a minute and talk about the "G" and the "M."

What is your character's goal? Not just for the purpose of the story you're writing—though knowing this is critical—but in *life*?

How have they been affected by the achievement of their Gs (goals) or by the inability to achieve them?

What are their Ms (motivations)? How was it born in the first place?

Because I know my characters so well, I can successfully answer these questions about their goals and motivations.

Let's start with the characters "Gs" and "Ms" within the context of the story we're writing. If you're a plotter, you'll have been meticulous about outlining this part. If you're a pantser, you'll figure it out sooner or later.

> ***Tip***
> *See the blank GMC chart in the character-building forms and tools chapter.

57

PATRICK "PIED" PIPER

A	Character Goal (In Story)	To win the affections of a woman and be pardoned for his historical sins.
B	Character Motivation (In Story)	He always gets whatever he wants and sees no reason why it shouldn't be the case this time. A witch has given him a challenge.

MAVERICK DANGERFIELD

A	Character Goal (In Story)	To date his therapist.
B	Character Motivation (In Story)	She's different. There's something about her that makes him feel complete. He's never been able to be himself with anyone else and not be judged.

ANDRÉS "REY" REINOSO

A	Character Goal (In Story)	To prevent his girlfriend from finding out his vile secret.
B	Character Motivation (In Story)	If she finds out his secret, he will lose her because of his ultimate betrayal.

These charts are simple, as they identify my characters' goals and motivations within the parameters of the story I'm going to write. I know this because I've taken the time to think about the plot and the story arc. These charts highlight the bare-boned facts about what is driving my character. This is the character's Open Self—the part the author immediately sees—the part your character tells you.

But what about the information we uncovered in our therapy sessions? What about the emotional themes? Remember, I said we *really* want to know our characters before the story begins. This means it's not enough to just know their goals and motivations within the context of the story. We need to consider their goals and motivations in life.

Think about the information your character revealed while in therapy. In addition to that, think about the psychological principles we discussed in chapter 4. Then deliberately apply those concepts to your character's goal and motivation in life.

PATRICK "PIED" PIPER

A	Character Goal (In Story)	To win the affections of a woman and be pardoned for his historical sins.
B	Character Motivation (In Story)	He always gets whatever he wants and sees no reason why it shouldn't be the case this time.
C	Character Goal (In Life)	To be validated for his time, energy, and efforts.
D	Character Motivation (In Life)	To prove to others that he is worthy of respect.

MAVERICK DANGERFIELD

A	Character Goal (In Story)	To date his therapist.
B	Character Motivation (In Story)	She's different. There's something about her that makes him feel complete. He's never been able to be himself around anyone else and not be judged.
C	Character Goal (In Life)	To have the respect of his colleagues and his mother.
D	Character Motivation (In Life)	He has something to prove, especially because his father suicided when he was a teenager.

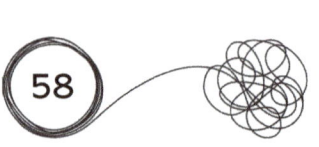

Applying Psychological Theory To Character Design

ANDRÉS "REY" REINOSO

A	Character Goal (In Story)	To prevent his girlfriend from finding out his vile secret
B	Character Motivation (In Story)	If she finds out his secret, he will lose her because of his ultimate betrayal.
C	Character Goal (In Life)	To be self-sufficient and brave.
D	Character Motivation (In Life)	He was so afraid when his father and sister were murdered. He never wants to feel like that again.

Now we're getting deeper, and our characters are becoming more 3D. These charts highlight the characters' motivations and goals within the plot, but they also consider these factors *outside* of the storyline—information I was able to gather from my therapy session with each of them.

For example, in addition to his goal to get the girl, we can see that, based on his historical experiences, Patrick's life goal is to be validated for his time, energy, and efforts. He is motivated by his deep need to prove to others that he is worthy of respect (**Chief Emotional Themes:** self-esteem, validation, unconditional positive regard).

Regarding Maverick, based on the information we obtained from his therapy session, we can deduce that, in addition to his goal to date his therapist, he also has a subconscious need to have the respect of his colleagues and his mother, a goal somehow related to the fact that his father died by suicide when he was a teenager (**Chief Emotional Themes:** abandonment, validation).

Finally, there's Rey. Because of the information we uncovered in his therapy session, we learned that, in addition to his story goal and motivation, in life, he values fearlessness. This motivation is connected to the fact that his father and sister were murdered before his very eyes when he was a young boy (**Chief Emotional Theme:** abandonment).

By continuing the therapy sessions, I'd be sure to uncover more information about each of these characters' relationships with their parents, their attachments, and their "selves"; however, for the purposes of this book, these are assumptions I can safely come to (because I've already told their tales).

All this rich information is valuable and will certainly allow us to begin the process of designing our 3D characters, but if we're really going to make our characters jump from the page, there's another layer we need to peel back. Specifically, the question of how **A x C and B x D** *intersect* needs to be considered.

In other words, what happens when Patrick's, Maverick's, and Andrés's lives and story goals collide?

How does this cross-section position them on the page of the story you're writing?

How does ***A x C, B x D*** shape their dialogue and the narrative as a whole?

This is the part of the writing that makes the story interesting. When creating 3D characters, it's not enough to simply highlight the goal and the motivation within the context of the story. The magic comes when we connect the story and life elements, weaving them into the conflict.

Now let's consider the conflict (and remember the psychological principles we fleshed out in chapter 4, as well as the juicy information we unearthed in our therapy sessions). Just as it's necessary to inject conflict into your story, to create 3D characters, it's also necessary to consider the ways psychological and emotional trauma might impact it.

The Psychology of Character Building for Authors

PATRICK "PIED" PIPER

A	Character Goal (In Story)	To win the affections of a woman and be pardoned for his historical sins.
B	Character Motivation (In Story)	He always gets whatever he wants and sees no reason why it shouldn't be the case this time.
C	Character Goal (In Life)	To be validated for his time, energy, and efforts.
D	Character Motivation (In Life)	To prove to others that he is worthy of respect.
E	Character Conflict (In Story)	Poor attachment style with parents (AT). Lack of trust in adults. This makes him unable to interact with people, (especially children and members of the opposite sex).
F	Character Conflict (In Life)	When he interacts with others (especially the love interest and her son) he is cocky, pompous and has no awareness of social cues.

Conflict x Psychology

His **Open Self** is confident, but it's clear that he's trying to keep his **Hidden Self** hidden. There's a lot going on with his **Unknown Self** (Johari's Window). Because of his attachment style, he is socially awkward, but this isn't his authentic self (**PCT**) This causes him to push his love interest away because he is afraid of rejection. He allows his subconscious fears to guide his present behavior (**Psychoanalysis – ID**). Developmentally, he is stuck on the third tier (**Belongingness and Love – Maslow's Hierarchy of Needs**)

Applying Psychological Theory To Character Design

MAVERICK DANGERFIELD

A	Character Goal (In Story)	To date his therapist.
B	Character Motivation (In Story)	She's different. There's something about her that makes him feel complete. He's never been able to be himself around anyone else and not be judged.
C	Character Goal (In Life)	To have the respect of his colleagues and his mother.
D	Character Motivation (In Life)	He has something to prove, especially because his father suicided when he was a teenager.
E	*Character Conflict (In Story)*	*He is unable to be truthful with his therapist because because he's afraid he won't be 'good enough' and will leave him, just like his father did.*
F	*Character Conflict (In Life)*	*He was traumatized by his father's suicide and developed abandonment and self-esteem issues.*

Conflict x Psychology

His **Open Self** is confident, but his **Unknown Self** is afraid (**Johari's Window**). Because his love interest is a therapist, she has access to his **Blind Self**. Because of poor relationship with his mother and the fact that his father suicided when he was a teenager, his **attachment style** is warped. The way he acts, and his potential are conflicted (**PCT**) but because he wants to date his therapist so badly, he makes a choice to respect her moral obligations. Interestingly, Maverick has **self-actualized** – he got the promotion he's been working so hard for (**Self Actualization - Maslow's Hierarchy of Needs**), but there's still a void in his life. What tier did he get stuck on?

The Psychology of Character Building for Authors

ANDRÉS "REY" REINOSO

A	Character Goal (In Story)	To prevent his girlfriend from finding out his vile secret
B	Character Motivation (In Story)	If she finds out his secret, he will lose her because of his ultimate betrayal.
C	Character Goal (In Life)	To be self-sufficient and brave.
D	Character Motivation (In Life)	He was so afraid when his father and sister were murdered. He never wants to feel like that again.
E	Character Conflict (In Story)	Because of his control issues, he is unable to be honest with the woman he loves.
F	Character Conflict (In Life)	Trauma & PTSD have caused him to use aggression and control as coping strategy. Unable to get in touch with important emotions (empathy, sympathy).

Conflict x Psychology

Andres's **Open Self** is confident, but his and based on his candidness, he has a level of awareness of the things going on in his **Unknown Self** (perhaps he's been to therapy before? - **Johari's Window**). The things that have happened to him in his past have forced him to behave a certain way (**CBT – Nature versus Nurture**). His thoughts about love are interesting (**CBT – ABC principle**). I wonder what will happen if he's shown unconditional positive regard… (**Emotional Themes**).

Do you see what I did?

First, I completed the chart by filling in the character's story conflict. Then I combined all the information I gathered with the nuggets I uncovered from my therapy session with each character. Then I started to apply some of the psychological principles to flesh each character's personality

out and highlight their life conflict. By engaging in this process, I created wonderful, psychological webs for my characters and made them into *real* people.

> ***Tip***
> Use the psychological GMC form in the Psychological Tools section to complete this process.

I didn't use all the psychological principles in these examples, but in real life, I might. This is because the deeper I go, the more 3D my characters become. To achieve this goal, I might use a form like this to keep track of the characters, the psychological theories, and the ways in which I apply them.

Psychological Application Form

Theory: Psychoanalysis
Character Name: Patrick 'Pied' Piper

Keywords:	Id, Ego, Superego; subconscious thoughts, desires.
	Quick Notes
1.	Controlled by his Id. This looks like him wearing his heart on his sleeve and being reactionary. Doesn't really care about others' emotions. Lacks empathy.
2.	Subconsciously he feels inferior but he doesn't know this. Maybe this ties into the concept of his hidden self.... (??)

Psychological Application Form

Theory: Johari Window
Character Name: Patrick 'Pied' Piper

Keywords:	Open, Blind, Hidden, Unknown Self
	Quick Notes
1.	Character's 'Open Self' is confident, I know this because of what I 'saw' in the therapy session; however, it is obvious he's trying to keep his 'Hidden self' hidden.
2.	'Blind Self' notes: Overbearing and authoritarian which might be his way of trying to keep others away from the truth of his pain (his horrible upbringing).

Again, the goal isn't to dump all of this into backstory, but rather the author's job is to present the character to the readers in a fresh and compelling way by skillfully using *show, don't tell* principles to make them pop off the page.

***

After your free-writing therapy session, complete these exercises. Use the blank worksheets in chapter 6 to facilitate the process:

1. Identify your character's archetype.

2. Identify your character's emotional theme(s). Make notes.

3. Identify where your character falls on Maslow's Hierarchy of Needs. Make notes about how this will be portrayed in your story.

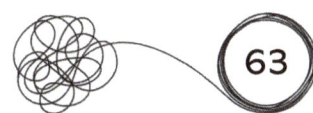

4. Complete the Johari Window for your character. Make notes about their Open, Blind, Hidden, and Unknown selves. Make notes about how this will show up in your story.

5. Are any of the other psychological principles highlighted in this book relevant? What are they? Make notes on the form.

6. What does the intersection look like at **A x C** and **B x D**?

7. Make notes about how this will show up in your story.

8. Write a short scene in which your character is speaking to another character about something that has upset them. Write it in first-person perspective.

9. Use the Life Story template in chapter 6 to free-write a story about your character's past and present.

CHAPTER RECAP

1. During your character therapy session, actively listen to what they say.

2. Watch their nonverbal cues and take notes about the ways in which it all adds up.

3. Don't stop listening until your character stops talking.

4. Consider the psychological principles and how they might apply to uncover all the hidden "gems."

5. Deliberately apply the gems to the story when creating conflict for your characters.

6. Let your imagination and your characters free.

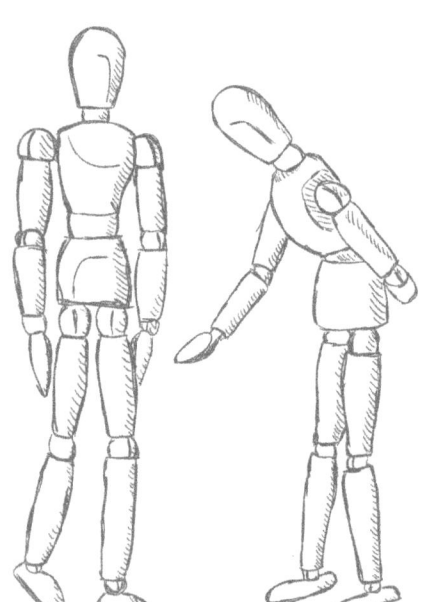

Pulling It Together

1. This concept is heavy, and, on the surface, it may seem like there are many moving parts, but the fact is once you engage in this process a few times, it will become like clockwork.

2. The following sections will help you pull it together so that it all flows seamlessly, like clockwork.

CONCLUSION

If you have given care and attention to the topics highlighted in this book, and if you've engaged in all of the exercises, I guarantee you'll be well on your way to successfully creating 3D characters who mimic real life. Not only that, but you should also have a working understanding of who your characters are *beyond* what they tell you (and others) they are, but the fun part is your characters were waiting for you to discover this information all along!

Here is a summary of what we've covered:

1. Discussed the foundational ideas of character design.

2. Highlighted the five emotional themes that can help up determine the Chief Emotional Theme governing our character's behavior.

3. Developed an understanding of the seven psychological principles that we can apply to our character-development process.

4. Conducted a therapy session with our character.

5. Developed our characters' story, life goals, and motivations, using the information we uncovered in our therapy sessions.

6. Considered **AxC/BxD** to deliberately layer the conflict with trauma.

It's not easy, and it may seem a bit cumbersome in the beginning, but I've tried to streamline the process with the hope that you'll be able to incorporate the elements into your character design practices. Some emotional themes and psychological theories will be more relevant for some characters than they are for others. Now that you have access to these strategies and tools, you can pick the ones that will assist in your character design process.

NB: *The goal is not for you to apply all of these ideas and concepts to every character you create. If this level of profound inquiry does not come naturally to you, it will only be a matter of time before it becomes tedious and unhelpful. Rather, the goal is to identify which ideas and techniques are relevant to your character and apply them for the purpose of making your character rich, dynamic, and 3D.*

STREAMLINING THE PROCESS

In an attempt to streamline this process, here is a suggested plan-of-attack for engaging your character on this level:

1. Use the character development questionnaire in the next section to develop a basic understanding of who your characters are (think: demographic/biopsychosocial).

2. Engage your characters in the therapy sessions to go deeper with them. Remember, give your imagination and characters permission to delve deeper into the exercise.

3. Based on what your characters "say" and how they "present themselves," revert to the psychological principles and see which apply. How will this manifest in your story? How will it create problems for your character? (Don't forget the GMC application—this is key!)

To approach character design in this way may seem unnatural at first, but the more you do it, the easier it becomes. Your characters will automatically begin to appear rich and layered because your eyes will be opened to their unlimited potential. By the time you conduct your therapy session and use the tools provided in the following chapter, you will have no choice but to paint your characters as the dynamic beings they always were.

When I think about the clients I've had over the years, I can easily recall the relief they experienced when they were finally able to connect the dots and make sense of their behavior. It was even better when they were able to find solutions to the conflict that have plagued them before they engaged in therapy.

Our characters are the same way.

They want to get to the bottom of things so that when they get to the climax of the story arc, the spot where they have to slay the formidable dragon, they've self-actualized and can come out victorious. By processing them on a deeper, 3D level, you're able to bring them to this wonderful end.

To effectively get them onto the page, you have to paint them vividly by taking all your research and penning it in a way that will resonate with your readers, thus forcing them to connect with your characters on deeper, intrinsic levels. As humans, we're wired to be affected by the suffering of others.

This is why readers read.

Conclusion

No matter the genre, readers want to see the likable hero defeat the monster, and when they realize they were abused by their parents or that they suffered some unimaginable loss at a critical point in their life, the readers are able to connect with them all the more. The trick is to feed this information to the reader in a way that taps into their subconscious sentiments.

Now it's up to you!

Get to know your characters and tell the stories *they* want you to tell.

Good luck, and happy writing.

> If you have questions, need assistance, or would like coaching in how to apply these principles, don't hesitate to email me at info@brooklyn-knightauthor.com

> *Character cannot be developed in ease and quiet. Only through experience of trial and suffering can the soul be strengthened, ambition inspired and success achieved.*

HELEN KELLER

Chapter 9

PSYCHOLOGICAL TOOLS

The key to writing a story that readers will never forget is to create 3D characters who leap off the page. The following documents are a selection of forms and tools you can use to assist with the development of your characters. What makes these forms special is that many of them are psychological assessments, which are used to assist clients in clinical assessments. Additionally, I developed some of the forms specifically to complement the topics covered in this book. Use these documents to flesh out your 3D characters and make them pop off the page.

DO NOT feel pressured to use every tool or concept highlighted in this book. Depending on your character, some tools will be more relevant than others. Ask each character the same questions and compare your notes to make predictions about how they will interact in your story.

*NB: Access to these tools **does not** permit you to conduct therapy, assessments, or evaluations of family, friends, or even pets. It takes years to obtain field-related credentials and practice outside of this scope is unethical.*

If you are in need of assistance, contact your local counseling agency.

Tools List

1. **Character Development Questionnaire:** a great character interview tool that can help you get to know your characters.

2. **Mental Status Exam:** use this tool to fully engage your imagination and examine your character's presentation in the therapy session; free-writing exercise.

3. **Triggers:** use this list to explore the root cause of your character's triggers.

4. **List of Emotions:** use this list of emotions to pinpoint your character's feelings.

5. **Anger Iceberg:** use this graphic to understand the factors underlying your character's "anger."

6. **Automatic Thoughts Chart:** help your character generate new thoughts, per the ABC theory.

7. **Johari Window:** explore your character's Open, Blind, Hidden, and Unknown Self.

8. **GMC Grid:** identify your character's goal, motivation, and conflict in the story and in life. Consider the cross-section between AxC and BxD.

9. **Stages of Change Graphic:** gain an understanding of the psychological/emotional changes your character goes through when they have to change their behavior.

10. **Life Story Templates:** pen a scene of your character's future and past.

11. **7 Characters Worksheet:** use this worksheet to determine if each of the seven characters are represented in your story.

12. **Chief Emotional Themes Worksheet:** which chief emotional themes impact your character? Use this worksheet to identify them.

13. **Psychological Theory Key Ideas:** a concise listing of the theories discussed and the ideas attached to each. Use this in conjunction with the psychological application form.

14. **Psychological Application Form:** track the psychological themes that impact your character and note the ways in which these issues will manifest in your story.

The Psychology of Character Building for Authors

Character Development Questionnaire

DEMOGRAPHIC INFORMATION

1. What is your character's full name (first, middle, last)?
2. Does your character have a nickname?
3. When was your character born?
4. How old is your character?
5. Which generation is your character part of (e.g., Gen X, Y, Z?)?
6. What is your character's zodiac sign?
7. What is your character's Chinese horoscope (sign/spirit animal)?

Author Questions
(Going Deeper)

- How does your character feel about their name/nickname?
- How did they get it?
- What is the meaning of the name?
- What culture did the name originate from?
- What events were happening (locally, nationally, and globally) the year your character was born?
- What implications might your character's "generation" have on their outlook in the story?
- What implications might your character's zodiac sign have on their personality?
- How does your character celebrate their birthday?

CHARACTER'S APPEARANCE

1. What is your character's ethnicity?
2. How tall is your character?
3. How much does your character weigh?
4. What is your character's build (muscular, stocky, large, etc.)?
5. What color are your character's eyes?
6. What color is your character's hair?
7. How long is your character's hair?
8. Does your character have scars/birthmarks?
9. Does your character have a physical disability?

Author Questions
(Going Deeper)

- Does your character's appearance impact their self-esteem? How?
- If your character has a disability, how does it impact the way they interact with others? How does it impact the way others interact with them?

APPAREL/STYLE

1. What is your character's casual dress style (hanging out with friends)?
2. What is your character's smart casual dress style (going to dinner/on a date)?
3. What does your character wear to bed?
4. Does your character have any special jewelry/accessories? How did they get them? Why are they meaningful?
5. What kind of shoes does your character wear?

Author Questions
(Going Deeper)

- How do other people view your character based on their style?
- If your character has special jewelry/accessories, how might this influence their personality?

FAMILY/RELATIONSHIPS

1. What are your character's parents' names, and how old are they?
2. What generation is your character's parents a part of?
3. Does your character have any siblings? If yes, how many?
4. What is your character's birth position in the family?
5. Does your character have any children? If yes, how many?
6. If your character has children, are they from the same union?
7. What kind of parent is your character?
8. How does your character feel about family events?
9. Does your character have a spouse/love interest?
10. Is your character married? For how long?
11. How did your character spend their honeymoon?
12. What was your character's first romantic encounter/kiss like?
13. How does your character display affection?
14. What is your character's love language[19] (Acts of Service, Gifts, Physical Touch, Words of Affirmation, Quality Time)?
15. What is your character's idea of the perfect date?
16. Has your character ever had their heart broken? If so, what happened?

Author Questions
(Going Deeper)

- Does your character have a good relationship with their siblings?
- How do the ages of your character's parents affect the character?
- How does your character's birth position affect them in your story?
- What is your character's relationship like with their children?
- How might the relationship they had with their parents affect their parenting style?
- If your character's children have different mothers/fathers, how does this affect the character relationship dynamic?
- What is the quality of your character's marriage/relationship?
- What is your character's love language?
- How might their first romantic encounter affect the story?
- If your character's heart has been broken, how might this affect the story?

FRIENDS/SOCIAL INTERACTIONS

1. How many close friends does your character have? Does your character have a best friend?
2. What does your character value most in friendship?

---

[19] Gary D. Chapman, 2002.

3. Does your character make friends easily? Why/why not?
4. What do people like about your character?
5. What don't people like about your character?
6. What does your character value most in a friendship?
7. Does your character have habits that annoy their friends?

Author Questions
(Going Deeper)

- What role does friendship (or the lack thereof) play in your character's life in your story?

HOME/LIVING ARRANGEMENTS

1. Where does your character live (country, state)?
2. For how long have they lived there?
3. If they moved locations, why?
4. What kind of accommodation does your character have (mansion, apartment, backseat of their car)?
5. How many cars does your character have?
6. Does your character have a roommate(s)? If yes, how many?
7. Does your character get along with the neighbors?
8. Does your character live in the suburbs or elsewhere?
9. What is the view outside of your character's window?
10. Does your character have a particular color scheme in their home?
11. What items are on your character's nightstand?
12. What is your character's most prized possession?

Author Questions
(Going Deeper)

- How does your character feel about their current living arrangements?
- How does your character feel about their roommates?
- Does where your character reside impact their personality?
- How do the neighbors impact your character?

CAREER/EDUCATION

1. What is your character's highest level of education?
2. What does your character do for a living?
3. Do they find this work enjoyable? Why/why not?
4. What things do they wish were different about their current profession?
5. What is your character's dream job?
6. What is your character's financial situation?
7. Is your character a miser or a spend-thrift?
8. What does your character spend most of their money on?
9. What would your character do if they hit the jackpot?

Psychological Tools

Author Questions
(Going Deeper)

- How does your character's job affect their outlook on life? Others?
- Why does/doesn't your character like their job?
- How does your character's financial status impact their outlook on life? Others?
- How does their educational attainment impact their outlook on life? Others?

LEISURE/TRAVEL

1. What does your character do on the weekends?
2. Where does your character like to go when they're alone?
3. Where does your character like to go with friends?
4. What are your character's favorite sports/hobbies?
5. Where would your character like to travel to?
6. How do they *like* to travel (private jet, commercial, limousine, bus, etc.)?
7. What are your character's lodging preferences (presidential suite, motel, cabin)?
8. How many languages does your character speak?
9. How many countries has your character visited?

Author Questions
(Going Deeper)

- What does your character's preferences of lodging and method of transportation say about their personality? How will this affect the story?
- How might your character's travel history impact their personality/the storyline? Their relationship with others?
- Where will your character (and readers) go during the story?

DIET

1. What is your character's favorite/comfort food? Why?
2. What food does your character hate? Why?
3. Does your character have any food allergies?
4. Does your character's religious beliefs impact what they can/cannot eat?
5. Does your character like to cook?
6. *Can* your character cook?

Author Questions
(Going Deeper)

- How might my character's diet impact them in your story?
- What memories are attached to your character's favorite/most hated foods?
- Why can/can't your character cook?
- What impact does their (in)ability to cook have on their relationships?

PETS

1. Does your character have a pet? If so, how many? If not, why?
2. What kind of pet does your character have?
3. How did your character obtain the pet?
4. What is the pet's name?
5. How would your character react if their pet died?
6. What is your character's favorite animal?

The Psychology of Character Building for Authors

Author Questions
(Going Deeper)
- What role will the pet play in the story?
- How does having a pet impact your character's personality?

MEDIA

1. Who is your character's favorite actors/actresses?
2. How often does your character watch movies/television?
3. Has your character ever been to the opera or a Broadway show?
4. What is your character's favorite music/songs (artists/bands)?
5. Has your character ever been to a live concert?
6. Does your character play any musical instruments? If so, which?
7. What is your character's favorite author/book?
8. What is your character's favorite genre?
9. What is your character's favorite quote?
10. How much time does your character spend using social media?
11. What is your character's favorite social media platform?
12. What is your character's least favorite social media platform?
13. Which social media app does your character use the most?
14. Which social media app does your character use the least?

Author Questions
(Going Deeper)
- What does your character's use of media mean about their personality?
- How might this impact the story?
- How does their favorite quote influence their behavior?

PERSONALITY/BEHAVIOR

1. Describe your character's personality in three words.
2. How does your character behave in public?
3. How does your character behave in private?
4. Is your character introverted or extroverted?
5. What does your character do when meeting someone for the first time?
6. How does your character interact with guests at a party?
7. How does your character feel about small talk?
8. How does your character feel about being the center of attention?
9. Is your character organized or disorganized?
10. Does your character tend to be forgetful/easily distracted?
11. Is your character more logical and analytical or more of a dreamer?
12. What is your character's favorite color?
13. Does your character have any pet peeves?
14. How does your character deal with feelings of anger?

Psychological Tools

15. How does your character handle everyday frustrations?
16. What is your character's greatest strength? How did they develop it?
17. What is your character's greatest weakness? How did they develop it?
18. What is something your character wishes they could do better?
19. What is your character's most embarrassing moment?
20. Does your character have any obsessions/addictions/vices?
21. Does your character neglect important responsibilities?
22. What makes your character happy?
23. What is your character most thankful for?
24. What does your character's "happy place" look like?
25. Does your character find happiness from within or look for it from external sources?

Author Questions
(Going Deeper)

- How will these aspects of the character's personality impact the story?
- Is there any psychological backstory that might impact the character's personality and behavior?
- How does this information affect how your character interacts with others?

VALUES/MORALS

1. How does your character feel about honesty?
2. Does your character believe in *always* telling the truth?
3. Does your character keep their promises?
4. Has there been a time when your character felt betrayed? What happened?
5. What is something your character would **never** do?
6. What is something people would be surprised to see your character do?
7. How does your character feel about rules and guidelines?
8. Is your character a leader or a follower?
9. Is your character religious/spiritual?
10. Does your character's religious beliefs differ from others close to them?
11. What is your character's political affiliations?
12. Does your character's political affiliations differ from others close to them?
13. When your character sees a beggar on the street, what do they do?
14. Does your character give to worthy causes?

Author Questions
(Going Deeper)

- How do your character's values and morals impact the way they interact with other characters in the story? How does this affect the storyline?
- How might your character's religious/spiritual convictions impact the story?
- How might your character's political affiliations impact the story?

7 CHARACTERS WORKSHEET

Which characters are represented in your story?
Are they all accounter for?

       NAME

PROTAGONIST		
ANTAGONIST		
DEUTERAGONIST (SIDEKICK)		
LOVE INTEREST		
MENTOR		
TERTIARY (FLAT) CHARACTER		
NARRATOR (1ST-/3RD-PERSON)		

7 CHARACTERS WORKSHEET

Which characters are represented in your story?
Are they all accounter for?

   NAME

PROTAGONIST		
ANTAGONIST		
DEUTERAGONIST (SIDEKICK)		
LOVE INTEREST		
MENTOR		
TERTIARY (FLAT) CHARACTER		
NARRATOR (1ST-/3RD-PERSON)		

7 CHARACTERS WORKSHEET

Which characters are represented in your story?
Are they all accounter for?

                    NAME

PROTAGONIST		
ANTAGONIST		
DEUTERAGONIST (SIDEKICK)		
LOVE INTEREST		
MENTOR		
TERTIARY (FLAT) CHARACTER		
NARRATOR (1ST-/3RD-PERSON)		

7 CHARACTERS WORKSHEET

Which characters are represented in your story?
Are they all accounter for?

                NAME

PROTAGONIST		
ANTAGONIST		
DEUTERAGONIST (SIDEKICK)		
LOVE INTEREST		
MENTOR		
TERTIARY (FLAT) CHARACTER		
NARRATOR (1ST-/3RD-PERSON)		

7 CHARACTERS WORKSHEET

Which characters are represented in your story?
Are they all accounter for?

       NAME

PROTAGONIST		
ANTAGONIST		
DEUTERAGONIST (SIDEKICK)		
LOVE INTEREST		
MENTOR		
TERTIARY (FLAT) CHARACTER		
NARRATOR (1ST-/3RD-PERSON)		

7 CHARACTERS WORKSHEET

Which characters are represented in your story?
Are they all accounter for?

		NAME
PROTAGONIST		
ANTAGONIST		
DEUTERAGONIST (SIDEKICK)		
LOVE INTEREST		
MENTOR		
TERTIARY (FLAT) CHARACTER		
NARRATOR (1ST-/3RD-PERSON)		

AUTOMATIC THOUGHTS

Your character's thoughts control the way they feel. Identify your character's negative thoughts and generate new, rational thoughts to impact the character and story arcs

Trigger	Automatic Thought	New Thought
E.g.: She's not speaking to me	She hates me	Maybe she's just having a bad day.

AUTOMATIC THOUGHTS

Your character's thoughts control the way they feel. Identify your character's negative thoughts and generate new, rational thoughts to impact the character and story arcs

Trigger	Automatic Thought	New Thought
E.g.: She's not speaking to me	She hates me	Maybe she's just having a bad day.

AUTOMATIC THOUGHTS

Your character's thoughts control the way they feel. Identify your character's negative thoughts and generate new, rational thoughts to impact the character and story arcs

Trigger	Automatic Thought	New Thought
E.g.: She's not speaking to me	She hates me	Maybe she's just having a bad day.

AUTOMATIC THOUGHTS

Your character's thoughts control the way they feel. Identify your character's negative thoughts and generate new, rational thoughts to impact the character and story arcs

Trigger	Automatic Thought	New Thought
E.g.: She's not speaking to me	She hates me	Maybe she's just having a bad day.

AUTOMATIC THOUGHTS

Your character's thoughts control the way they feel. Identify your character's negative thoughts and generate new, rational thoughts to impact the character and story arcs

Trigger	Automatic Thought	New Thought
E.g.: She's not speaking to me	She hates me	Maybe she's just having a bad day.

AUTOMATIC THOUGHTS

Your character's thoughts control the way they feel. Identify your character's negative thoughts and generate new, rational thoughts to impact the character and story arcs

Trigger	Automatic Thought	New Thought
E.g.: She's not speaking to me	She hates me	Maybe she's just having a bad day.

CHIEF EMOTIONAL THEMES

What Chief Emotional Themes color your character's view on life and relationships? What evidence do you have of this?

                          EVIDENCE

UNCONDITIONAL POSITIVE REGARD ISSUES		1. 2. 3.
VALIDATION ISSUES		1. 2. 3.
SELF-WORTH ISSUES		1. 2. 3.
INFLATED EGO ISSUES		1. 2. 3.
ABANDONMENT ISSUES		1. 2. 3.

CHIEF EMOTIONAL THEMES

What Chief Emotional Themes color your character's view on life and relationships? What evidence do you have of this?

     EVIDENCE

UNCONDITIONAL POSITIVE REGARD ISSUES		1. 2. 3.
VALIDATION ISSUES		1. 2. 3.
SELF-WORTH ISSUES		1. 2. 3.
INFLATED EGO ISSUES		1. 2. 3.
ABANDONMENT ISSUES		1. 2. 3.

CHIEF EMOTIONAL THEMES

What Chief Emotional Themes color your character's view on life and relationships? What evidence do you have of this?

                    EVIDENCE

UNCONDITIONAL POSITIVE REGARD ISSUES		1. 2. 3.
VALIDATION ISSUES		1. 2. 3.
SELF-WORTH ISSUES		1. 2. 3.
INFLATED EGO ISSUES		1. 2. 3.
ABANDONMENT ISSUES		1. 2. 3.

CHIEF EMOTIONAL THEMES

What Chief Emotional Themes color your character's view on life and relationships? What evidence do you have of this?

    EVIDENCE

UNCONDITIONAL POSITIVE REGARD ISSUES		1. 2. 3.
VALIDATION ISSUES		1. 2. 3.
SELF-WORTH ISSUES		1. 2. 3.
INFLATED EGO ISSUES		1. 2. 3.
ABANDONMENT ISSUES		1. 2. 3.

CHIEF EMOTIONAL THEMES

What Chief Emotional Themes color your character's view on life and relationships? What evidence do you have of this?

                    EVIDENCE

THEME	✓	EVIDENCE
UNCONDITIONAL POSITIVE REGARD ISSUES		1. 2. 3.
VALIDATION ISSUES		1. 2. 3.
SELF-WORTH ISSUES		1. 2. 3.
INFLATED EGO ISSUES		1. 2. 3.
ABANDONMENT ISSUES		1. 2. 3.

CHIEF EMOTIONAL THEMES

What Chief Emotional Themes color your character's view on life and relationships? What evidence do you have of this?

                      EVIDENCE

	✓	EVIDENCE
UNCONDITIONAL POSITIVE REGARD ISSUES		1. 2. 3.
VALIDATION ISSUES		1. 2. 3.
SELF-WORTH ISSUES		1. 2. 3.
INFLATED EGO ISSUES		1. 2. 3.
ABANDONMENT ISSUES		1. 2. 3.

	Known to Self	Unknown to self
Known to others	**Open Self** NOTES	**Blind Self** NOTES
Unknown to Others	**Hidden Self** NOTES	**Unknown Self** NOTES

	Known to Self	Unknown to self
Known to others	**Open Self** NOTES	**Blind Self** NOTES
Unknown to Others	**Hidden Self** NOTES	**Unknown Self** NOTES

	Known to Self	Unknown to self
Known to others	**Open Self** NOTES	**Blind Self** NOTES
Unknown to Others	**Hidden Self** NOTES	**Unknown Self** NOTES

	Known to Self	Unknown to self
Known to others	**Open Self** NOTES	**Blind Self** NOTES
Unknown to Others	**Hidden Self** NOTES	**Unknown Self** NOTES

	Known to Self	Unknown to self
Known to others	**Open Self** NOTES	**Blind Self** NOTES
Unknown to Others	**Hidden Self** NOTES	**Unknown Self** NOTES

	Known to Self	Unknown to self
Known to others	**Open Self** NOTES	**Blind Self** NOTES
Unknown to Others	**Hidden Self** NOTES	**Unknown Self** NOTES

Psychological
Application Form

Theory: _____

Character Name: _____

Keywords:

Quick Notes

Psychological
Application Form

Theory: _____

Character Name: _____

Keywords:

Quick Notes

Psychological
Application Form

Theory: _____

Character Name: _____

Keywords:

Quick Notes

Psychological
Application Form

Theory: _____

Character Name: _____

Keywords:

Quick Notes

Psychological
Application Form

Theory: _____

Character Name: _____

Keywords:

Quick Notes

Psychological Application Form

Theory: _____

Character Name: _____

Keywords:

Quick Notes

Psychological
Application Form

Theory: _____

Character Name: _____

Keywords:

Quick Notes

Psychological
Application Form

Theory: _____

Character Name: _____

Keywords:

Quick Notes

Psychological
Application Form

Theory: _____

Character Name: _____

Keywords:

Quick Notes

Psychological
Application Form

Theory: _____

Character Name: _____

Keywords:

Quick Notes

Goal, Motivation, Conflict Worksheet

Character Name:

A	Character Goal (In Life)	
B	Character Goal (In Story)	
C	Character Motivation (In Life)	
D	Character Motivation (In Story)	
E	Character Conflict (In Life)	
F	Character Conflict (In Story)	

Goal, Motivation, Conflict Worksheet

Character Name:

A	Character Goal (In Life)	
B	Character Goal (In Story)	
C	Character Motivation (In Life)	
D	Character Motivation (In Story)	
E	Character Conflict (In Life)	
F	Character Conflict (In Story)	

Goal, Motivation, Conflict Worksheet

Character Name:

A	Character Goal (In Life)	
B	Character Goal (In Story)	
C	Character Motivation (In Life)	
D	Character Motivation (In Story)	
E	Character Conflict (In Life)	
F	Character Conflict (In Story)	

Goal, Motivation, Conflict Worksheet

Character Name:

A	Character Goal (In Life)	
B	Character Goal (In Story)	
C	Character Motivation (In Life)	
D	Character Motivation (In Story)	
E	Character Conflict (In Life)	
F	Character Conflict (In Story)	

Goal, Motivation, Conflict Worksheet

Character Name:

A	Character Goal (In Life)	
B	Character Goal (In Story)	
C	Character Motivation (In Life)	
D	Character Motivation (In Story)	
E	Character Conflict (In Life)	
F	Character Conflict (In Story)	

Goal, Motivation, Conflict Worksheet

Character Name:

A	Character Goal (In Life)	
B	Character Goal (In Story)	
C	Character Motivation (In Life)	
D	Character Motivation (In Story)	
E	Character Conflict (In Life)	
F	Character Conflict (In Story)	

Goal, Motivation, Conflict Worksheet

Character Name:

A	Character Goal (In Life)	
B	Character Goal (In Story)	
C	Character Motivation (In Life)	
D	Character Motivation (In Story)	
E	Character Conflict (In Life)	
F	Character Conflict (In Story)	

Goal, Motivation, Conflict Worksheet

Character Name:

A	Character Goal (In Life)	
B	Character Goal (In Story)	
C	Character Motivation (In Life)	
D	Character Motivation (In Story)	
E	Character Conflict (In Life)	
F	Character Conflict (In Story)	

Goal, Motivation, Conflict Worksheet

Character Name:

A	Character Goal (In Life)	
B	Character Goal (In Story)	
C	Character Motivation (In Life)	
D	Character Motivation (In Story)	
E	Character Conflict (In Life)	
F	Character Conflict (In Story)	

Goal, Motivation, Conflict Worksheet

Character Name:

A	Character Goal (In Life)	
B	Character Goal (In Story)	
C	Character Motivation (In Life)	
D	Character Motivation (In Story)	
E	Character Conflict (In Life)	
F	Character Conflict (In Story)	

CHARACTER ARC TRACKING FORM

Use this form to make notes about your characters beliefs/presentation at the various points:

Character Arc Type

Growth ☐   Transformation ☐   Fall ☐

Character Name: _____

Character Role: _____

_____
_____
_____
_____
_____
_____
_____
_____
_____
_____
_____
_____

CHARACTER ARC TRACKING FORM

Use this form to make notes about your characters beliefs/presentation at the various points:

Character Arc Type

Growth ☐   Transformation ☐   Fall ☐

Character Name: _____

Character Role: _____

_____

_____

_____

_____

_____

_____

_____

_____

_____

_____

_____

_____

CHARACTER ARC TRACKING FORM

Use this form to make notes about your characters beliefs/presentation at the various points:

Character Arc Type

Growth ☐   Transformation ☐   Fall ☐

Character Name: _____

Character Role: _____

_____

_____

_____

_____

_____

_____

_____

_____

_____

_____

_____

CHARACTER ARC TRACKING FORM

Use this form to make notes about your characters beliefs/presentation at the various points:

Character Arc Type

Growth ☐   Transformation ☐   Fall ☐

Character Name: _____

Character Role: _____

_____

_____

_____

_____

_____

_____

_____

_____

_____

_____

_____

CHARACTER ARC TRACKING FORM

Use this form to make notes about your characters beliefs/presentation at the various points:

Character Arc Type

Growth ☐   Transformation ☐   Fall ☐

Character Name: _____

Character Role: _____

CHARACTER ARC TRACKING FORM

Use this form to make notes about your characters beliefs/presentation at the various points:

Character Arc Type

Growth ☐   Transformation ☐   Fall ☐

Character Name: _____

Character Role: _____

_____

_____

_____

_____

_____

_____

_____

_____

_____

_____

_____

TRIGGERS

Definition: A stimulus (person, place, situation or this) that produces unwanted emotional or behavioral responses.

THE PROBLEM
Describe the problem your character's triggers are producing.
What's the worst thing that could happen if they are exposed to their triggers?

_____

_____

_____

Trigger Catagories
Anything can be a trigger. To explore your character's triggers, think about each oth the categories listed below. List your responses in the space provided.

EMOTION STATE/THOUGHTS	
PEOPLE	
PLACES	
THINGS	
ACTIVITES/ SITUATIONS	

TRIGGERS

Definition: A stimulus (person, place, situation or this) that produces unwanted emotional or behavioral responses.

THE PROBLEM
Describe the problem your character's triggers are producing.
What's the worst thing that could happen if they are exposed to their triggers?

_____
_____
_____

Trigger Catagories
Anything can be a trigger. To explore your character's triggers, think about each oth the categories listed below. List your responses in the space provided.

EMOTION STATE/THOUGHTS	
PEOPLE	
PLACES	
THINGS	
ACTIVITES/ SITUATIONS	

TRIGGERS

Definition: A stimulus (person, place, situation or this) that produces unwanted emotional or behavioral responses.

THE PROBLEM
Describe the problem your character's triggers are producing.
What's the worst thing that could happen if they are exposed to their triggers?

_____

_____

_____

_____

Trigger Catagories
Anything can be a trigger. To explore your character's triggers, think about each oth the categories listed below. List your responses in the space provided.

EMOTION STATE/THOUGHTS	
PEOPLE	
PLACES	
THINGS	
ACTIVITES/ SITUATIONS	

TRIGGERS

Definition: A stimulus (person, place, situation or this) that produces unwanted emotional or behavioral responses.

THE PROBLEM
Describe the problem your character's triggers are producing.
What's the worst thing that could happen if they are exposed to their triggers?

_____

_____

_____

_____

Trigger Catagories
Anything can be a trigger. To explore your character's triggers, think about each oth the categories listed below. List your responses in the space provided.

EMOTION STATE/THOUGHTS	
PEOPLE	
PLACES	
THINGS	
ACTIVITES/ SITUATIONS	

TRIGGERS

Definition: A stimulus (person, place, situation or this) that produces unwanted emotional or behavioral responses.

THE PROBLEM
Describe the problem your character's triggers are producing.
What's the worst thing that could happen if they are exposed to their triggers?

_____

_____

_____

_____

Trigger Catagories
Anything can be a trigger. To explore your character's triggers, think about each oth the categories listed below. List your responses in the space provided.

EMOTION STATE/THOUGHTS	
PEOPLE	
PLACES	
THINGS	
ACTIVITES/ SITUATIONS	

TRIGGERS

Definition: A stimulus (person, place, situation or this) that produces unwanted emotional or behavioral responses.

THE PROBLEM
Describe the problem your character's triggers are producing.
What's the worst thing that could happen if they are exposed to their triggers?

_____

_____

_____

Trigger Catagories
Anything can be a trigger. To explore your character's triggers, think about each oth the categories listed below. List your responses in the space provided.

EMOTION STATE/THOUGHTS	
PEOPLE	
PLACES	
THINGS	
ACTIVITES/ SITUATIONS	

LIFE STORY

Free-write excercise
The Past & The Future

Write the story of your character's past.

LIFE STORY

Free-write excercise
The Past & The Future

Write the story of your character's past.

LIFE STORY

Free-write excercise
The Past & The Future

Write the story of your character's past.

LIFE STORY

Free-write excercise
The Past & The Future

Write the story of your character's past.

LIFE STORY

Free-write excercise
The Past & The Future

Write the story of your character's past.

LIFE STORY

Free-write excercise
The Past & The Future

Write the story of your character's past.

LIFE STORY

Free-write excercise
The Past & The Future

Write the story of your character's past.

LIFE STORY

Free-write excercise
The Past & The Future

Write the story of your character's past.

LIFE STORY

Free-write excercise
The Past & The Future

Write the story of your character's past.

LIFE STORY

Free-write excercise
The Past & The Future

Write the story of your character's past.

MENTAL STATUS EXAM

Use this form during your free-write therapy session to get a clear picture of your character's presentation.

Client Name				Date		
OBSERVATIONS						
Appearance	☐ Neat	☐ Disheveled	☐ Inappropriate	☐ Bizarre		☐ Other
Speech	☐ Normal	☐ Tangential	☐ Pressured	☐ Impoverished		☐ Other
Eye Contact	☐ Normal	☐ Intense	☐ Avoidant	☐ Other		
Motor Activity	☐ Normal	☐ Restless	☐ Tics	☐ Slowed		☐ Other
Affect	☐ Full	☐ Constricted	☐ Flat	☐ Labile		☐ Other
Comments:						
MOOD						
☐ Euthymic	☐ Anxious	☐ Angry	☐ Depressed	☐ Euphoric	☐ Irritable	☐ Other
Comments:						
COGNITION						
Orientation Impairment	☐ None	☐ Place	☐ Object	☐ Person		☐ Time
Memory Impairment	☐ None	☐ Short-Term	☐ Long-Term	☐ Other		
Attention	☐ Normal	☐ Distracted	☐ Other			
Comments:						
PERCEPTION						
Hallucinations	☐ None	☐ Auditory	☐ Visual	☐ Other		
Other	☐ None	☐ Derealization	☐ Depersonalization			
Comments:						
THOUGHTS						
Suicidality	☐ None	☐ Ideation	☐ Plan	☐ Intent		☐ Self-Harm
Homicidality	☐ None	☐ Aggressive	☐ Intent	☐ Plan		
Delusions	☐ None	☐ Grandiose	☐ Paranoid	☐ Religious		☐ Other
Comments:						
BEHAVIOR						
☐ Cooperative	☐ Guarded	☐ Hyperactive	☐ Agitated			☐ Paranoid
☐ Stereotyped	☐ Aggressive	☐ Bizarre	☐ Withdrawn			☐ Other
Comments:						
INSIGHT	☐ Good	☐ Fair	☐ Poor	Comments:		
JUDGMENT	☐ Good	☐ Fair	☐ Poor	Comments:		

LIST OF EMOTIONS

Amazed	Foolish	Overwhelmed
Angry	Frustrated	Peaceful
Annoyed	Furious	Proud
Anxious	Grieving	Relieved
Ashamed	Happy	Resentful
Bitter	Hopeful	Sad
Bored	Hurt	Satisfied
Comfortable	Inadequate	Scared
Confused	Insecure	Self-conscious
Content	Inspired	Shocked
Depressed	Irritated	Silly
Determined	Jealous	Stupid
Disdain	Joy	Suspicious
Disgusted	Lonely	Tense
Eager	Lost	Terrified
Embarrassed	Loving	Trapped
Energetic	Miserable	Uncomfortable
Envious	Motivated	Worried
Excited	Nervous	Worthless

THE EMOTIONS UNDERNEATH ANGER

ANGER

FRUSTRATION   FEAR   INSECURITY
GUILT   HELPLESSNESS   TIRED
INADEQUACY   SHAME   STRESS
LONELINESS   DISAPPOINTED
HUNGER   EMPTINESS
JEALOUS   SADNESS
HURT   THREATENED
ANXIETY
PAIN

Stages of Change

1 — **Pre-contemplation**: The character doesn't recognize the severity of the problem and is not ready to change. They may have tried before and given up.

2 — **Contemplation**: The character is starting to think about changing because they notice problems. They are still not sure and the behaior continues.

3 — **Preparation**: The character has decided to change their problem behavior and is making plans. They are making small changes but might still have the problem.

4 — **Action**: Major steps are taken to end the problem behavior. The character is avoiding triggers and seeking help.

5 — **Maintenance**: The changes the character made during the Action stage and consistent. They may still experience temptation, but they have adopted new behaviors.

Relapse: Sometimes the character may fall back into bad behavior. This can happen at any stage.

AUTHOR BIO

Letitia R. Washington graduated with her bachelors in psychology (minor in sociology) in 2005 and her master's in clinical mental health counseling in April 2012. She has worked as a probation officer and a drug and alcohol assessor for the Bermuda government, and as a credentialed clinical mental health counselor in clinical, school, and private settings.

Letitia is also a best-selling romance author who writes under the pen name "Brooklyn Knight." In 2018, she quit her PhD in counselor education and supervision to focus on her writing career; and in 2021, she left her full-time job to formerly establish Brooklyn Knight Enterprises, where she offers author coaching services for both aspiring and experienced writers, using a creative blend of her clinical and writing experience.

REFERENCES

Association., A. P. (2013). *Diagnostic and statistical manual of mental disorders (5th ed.).* Retrieved from https://doi-org.ezproxy.frederick.edu/10.1176/appi.books.9780890425596.

Berland, A. (Ed.) (2017). *Using Johari Window to Explore Patient and Provider Perspectives.* International Journal of Health Governance, 22(1), 47-51.

Bolen, R. (2000). *Validity of Attachent Theory.* Trauma, Violence, & Abuse, 1(2), 128-153.

Boynton, T. (2001). *Applied Research Using Alpha/Theta Training for Enhancing Creativity and Well-Being.* Journal of Neurotherapy, 5(1-2), 5-18, doi. 10.1300/J184v05n01_02

Clark, V. (2010). *CBT for Beginners.* Drug and Alcohol Review, 29(2).

Corballis, M. (2014). *Left Brain, Right Brain: Facts and Fantasies.* PLoS Biology, 12(1).

Eagly, A. &. (2013). *The Nature–Nurture Debates.* Perspectives on Psychological Science, 8(3), 240-357.

Ellis, A. (2005). *The Revised ABC's of rational-emotive therapy (RET).* Journal of Rational-Emotive & Cognitive-Behavior Therapy, 9(3), 139-172.

D. Chapman, G. (2022). The Five Love Languages: How to Express Heartfelt

Commitment to Your Mate. (n.p.): Lulu.com.

References

Henry Ford Quotes. (n.d.). BrainyQuote. Retrieved February 23, 2021, from https://www.brainy-quote.com/quotes/henry_ford_383662#:%7E:text=Henry%20Ford%20Quotes&text=Please%20enable%20Javascript-,There%20are%20no%20big%20problems%2C%20there%20are,a%20lot%20of%20little%20problems.

Kupfersmid., J. (2019). *Freud's Clincal Theories Then and Now.* Psychodynamic Psychiatry, 47(1), 81-97

Lester, D. (2013). *Measuring Maslow's Hierarchy of Needs.* Psychological Reports, 113(1), 15-17.

Masters, J. (1981). *Developmental Psychology.* Annual Review of Psychology, 32(1), 117-151.

Narknisorn, B. (2012). *Person-Centered Therapy and Personal Growth.* Journal of Social and Development Sciences, 3(9), 322-330.

Nerher, A. (1996). *Jung's Theory of Archetypes: A Critique.* Journal of Humanistic Psychology, 36 (2, 61-91).